THE ART OF CONSPIRACY
Hidden in Plain Sight

Ruling families and monarchies, also known as The Khazarian Mafia, have been consolidating their illusion of power and control for centuries. The culmination of which has brought us to the apex of their jurisdiction which is now in the process of imploding on itself.

KIRK GALBRAITH

The Art of Conspiracy / Kirk Galbraith
First Edition

Publisher: Platypus Publishing

DISCLAIMER

We live in a time where lawyers, doctors, politicians and many other professionals are compromised to the point where everyone's right of freedom to speak their own opinions, thoughts and conclusions is censored. Therefore the author, publisher and all those involved in the distribution of this book present the information for consideration and entertainment purposes only. These are simply the author's experiences, opinions and perspective, so please do your own research to connect the dots for yourself. Be aware that none of the information in this work is meant to be advice, nor is it meant to diagnose, treat, heal or prevent anyone from any ailment or disease. Please consult your physician for advice on a medical condition.

DEDICATION

This book is dedicated to all the freedom fighters across the world, and from all walks of life, who have felt that their voice was not heard. You spoke out with friends and at family gatherings or social media and may have been ridiculed, shunned, alienated and even ostracized as a result. Always remember that your words made an impression on the universal consciousness, and it has made a difference. Thank you for your courage!

ACKNOWLEDGEMENTS

My deepest thanks are to Matt Rudnitsky of Platypus Publishing for his inspiring leadership and encouragement without which I probably would not have thought this writing a possibility, let alone its manifestation.

Also heartfelt thanks to my friend Autumn Villard who spent countless hours consulting, sharing ideas and opinions with me.

And to my wonderful wife and favorite golfing partner Elizabeth for all her unwavering love and support.

Thank you, babe.

TABLE OF CONTENTS

INTRODUCTION

"All truth passes through three stages. First, it is ridiculed. Second, it is violently opposed. Third, it is accepted as being self-evident."

~ *Arthur Schopenhauer* ~

Systemic fraud has plagued humanity and our earth for thousands of years! The author shows how the fraud snaked its way into societies via banking, legal, military and medical systems. It then grew tentacles through political and media institutions and is choking our life out from within. Then we will take a look at restoring the planet and her people to health and prosperity with solutions that make those antiquated systems obsolete.

It's one thing to know of corruption in politics and religion, but when it seeps into your life like an insidious hellion who is intent on stealing your energy and tracking your every desire, it's time to wake up and slay the dragon.

If you have recently begun to see through the veil of deceit, but have not been able to connect the dots, the ideas and concepts in this short book are the culmination of 42 years of research to help bring it all together. In this synopsis there are many references to books and links to websites with more comprehensive studies and descriptions on each topic, for those who want to dig deeper.

Chapter 1

LAWFUL VS LEGAL:
NATURAL OR STATUTES

"The only difference between a tax man and a taxidermist is that the taxidermist leaves the skin."

~ *Mark Twain* ~

We entered the courtroom, some new friends and family and me. A cold and lifeless place with a very low frequency energy that induces fear and cowardice. My former wife and in-laws were there because I naively convinced them that this would be another victory similar to my first appearance. My friends were there because they too were hoping I would put the Canada Revenue agent in his place again.

Oh, such folly when we entertain imaginings that we "useless eaters," a name we are referred to by the ruling elite, would overcome one of their many systems. I had done enough research to see the ruse, but definitely was not sufficiently armed with all the tricks of Maritime Admiralty Law to navigate my way around a courtroom.

You see, the first time I went to court when they called the Canada Revenue Agency (CRA) agent to testify, I had the opportunity to cross examine.

Kirk: "Mr. White, do you recall coming to my house?"

Mr. White: "Yes."

Kirk: "And when I opened the door, what did you say?"

Mr. White: "I am Mr. White from the Canada Revenue Agency. Are you Kirk Galbraith?"

Kirk: "And did I then begin to close the door and say, I do not need to talk to you!"?

Mr. White: "Yes."

Kirk: "And did you have Failure to File a T4 Income Tax papers to serve me?"

Mr. White: "Yes."

Kirk: "And then did you throw those very papers on the floor inside the door?"

Mr. White: "Yes."

Had I known what I was doing I would have made a motion to dismiss the case, albeit based on the technicality of improper serving of papers. They are supposed to identify you and then physically hand you the papers.

But the Crown attorney interjected, requesting we adjourn and make another date. The administrator (judge) sitting on the bench (bank) of the Crown then said I was free to go which brought cheers from my friends in the audience, and we clustered in the hallway outside the courtroom where lawyers were wondering what all the celebrating was about.

I would have had no problem getting off on a technicality because I know beyond a shadow of a doubt that income tax collection is unlawful and does not help pay for all the wonderful services we enjoy. If you look up and do the math on the gas tax for 3.7 million vehicles in British Columbia, that alone could easily pay for our utilities. So no, income tax collections do not pay for services, instead they fund the opulence enjoyed by the Vatican and the Queen's Royal Estates (where the term real estate is derived from).

The IRS and CRA are not agencies of their respective governments, rather they are private corporations and legal agencies of the International Monetary Fund (IMF) and the World Bank. That is where the federal taxes are sent for distribution to their corporate bosses.

Legal and lawful are two very different terms. The former was devised to enslave us by binding everything we are trained to do, to man- made statutes. The latter falls under Natural Law which encompasses the "nonaggression principle," our God given freedoms and unalienable rights. I like to think of unalienable as not being able to put a lien on it and therefore non-taxable.

And there is the more complex intertwining of our relationships involved with the writing of hundreds of statutes per day to convolute and confuse our dealings. This makes it near impossible to conduct our affairs without hiring a British Accredited Registry (BAR) agent or lawyer.

The Natural or Divine Law reality that we are currently choosing to manifest, in order to make the old-world order obsolete, has only one primary directive which, simply put, is Do no harm, loss or injury to person or property which encompasses everything we may encounter in our daily transactions and will make things very simple. When there are more complex situations that need adjudication such as "self defense" a Grand Jury of our peers can be formed, the cases heard and remedy brought to resolution in a timely manner. In a lawful world, and at our full-time jobs, we receive compensation for our labor with money in exchange for products and services. And since that exchange is of equal value there is no real gain, therefore no income so no income tax. Income tax can only be lawfully applied on investments where there is an increase over and above the initial capital outlay.

Our birth certificate bonds are where the funds come from for our mortgages, and all other loans, and our signature creates the money. More on this in chapter 2.

How many times have I asked myself if I only knew then what I know now?

So next time when we were waiting for the court to start, Mr. White came to me and handed me the papers and said, "Kirk Galbraith, you're served."

Whoops! Fighting back a terrible feeling that I was in deep shit now, I said, "You should find another job! The CRA is going down!"

I still believe that statement today, 20 years later. We are making headway as the global consciousness awakens to corruption worldwide, becoming more and more obvious as the powers that shouldn't be, reveal their hand.

So this time, when my name was called to come forward, I knew that if I opened the gate and walked through, I would be in their jurisdiction. I stated that I would stay where I was, and the black robed priest, the administrator seated at the bench, beckoned me to enter. I declined but he persisted, saying that I could not be heard where I was, to which I replied I will speak louder. We bantered back and forth until his patience ran out and he ordered the Sheriffs to take me downstairs to the underground holding cell.

To my surprise and considerable embarrassment, they strip-searched me, and wouldn't you know they didn't find my T4 Tax Return stuffed up my butt!

Now inside the holding cell, I started to walk back and forth because, after all, isn't that what they do in the movies? Oh please! It seemed rather futile. I was in that little cell for about 15-20 minutes, and I have to admit the only resource left at that point was prayer.

Next, the Sheriff gave me back my clothes and took me back up to the courtroom. So now the black robed priest of Moloch asked me if I would cross over to his jurisdiction to which I said, "For the record, I am coming in under duress." Now that he had me where he needed me, we adjourned for several months in the future.

This gave me the time I needed to make inquiries within the "freedom movement" and I found a brilliant young man who knows more Canadian history law than most lawyers, and he even knew the court procedures to put it all together. Now I felt we could win by showing how it all started, when in 1919, they dropped the word War from the Income War Tax Act (1917). The Act was initially instituted as a temporary tax to pay for the war requiring voluntary payments by those earning more than $3000.00. A stroke of the pen changed all that when it became the Income Tax Act and the rates have been going up ever since.

And by the way, the war was funded on both sides by the Rothschilds' a tactic the family has always used to gain more control over lands and kingdoms and people. Although this family is not at the top of the food chain, they are responsible for much of the misery, bloodshed and oppression of mankind, to this day.

Our evidence encompassed many decades of case law and Acts passed such as The Statute of Westminster 1931, but this simple overview is not meant to contain the volumes of research we used.

The Bank of Canada, the only bank in the world known as the "Peoples Bank," functioned more properly in the early days, creating money almost interest free. This enabled Canadians to build the St. Lawrence Seaway, the Trans Canada Highway, Hospitals, Airports and much of our infrastructure.

In 1974 Prime Minister Pierre Elliott Trudeau made the unilateral decision to stop using the Bank of Canada to create our money. He decided we would now need to pay interest on borrowed money from a privately owned bank outside of Canada, the Bank for International Settlements (BIS) in Switzerland.

See Figure 1: which shows how our debt skyrocketed after that, lining the pockets of his bankster buddies and putting us into a debt slave system.

This is one of the many control mechanisms to keep us busy with survival which leaves many tired at the end of the day just to flop in front of the propaganda box, where we are entertained with our favorite sports and shows.

Anyway, David put together a winning case for me and a few others in the movement at the time. When the court date came and we presented the evidence that income taxation was fraud and unlawful, the Crown looked at his superior perplexed and knowing this meant defeat, they adjourned.

At our next court date they read a fax from the Minister of Finance saying that my friend could no longer represent me, and the few other defendants at the time because he was practicing law without a license. Even in their own Statute Laws which are man- made legalese, it clearly states that anyone can have anybody represent them.

It was at that moment that I became aware that these tyrants care not about law or what is right and just. They only care that they win at all costs, like any true narcissist bully.

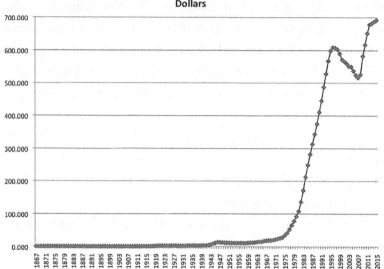

Figure 1: Federal Government Net Debt, 1867-2015, Billions of Dollars

My journey began in the mid 70s after I had been anesthetizing myself with alcohol on a daily basis in an attempt to live a carefree and fun loving lifestyle and not having to contemplate heavy subject matter. It was at the tender age of 21 when I began reading the book *None Dare Call It Conspiracy* by Gary Allen. The information was so scary and almost unbelievable that I had to put it down after the first few chapters as I was entering the realm of "cognitive dissonance" where two opposing beliefs cannot be held in the mind at once. The dominant belief is usually introduced by a constant and unrelenting repetition. The education and multimedia systems make it very difficult to entertain the opposing or dissonant belief. The prime example in society today is that we have elected authority figures and we trust that they have our best interests at heart. To entertain any opposing belief immediately conjures up a reinforced state of fear that renders the mind unwilling to think more critically. A prerequisite to counter cognitive dissonance is first an open mind. One must be willing to take an honest look at topics that are outside of their current comfort zone of formulated ideas and opinions and couple that with the ability to actually change those ideas and opinions when new knowledge is revealed or there is better comprehension from a more informed source.

But it is much safer to go along to get along because it is frightening to think that we are not in control of our own lives and that our representatives are following a heinous agenda that is far from in favor of our best interests.

Thus I was unable to process how controlled we are on this planet. It felt like our karmic consequences were now playing out in a sentence to life on earth.

Losing in court to a system made up of liars and cheats is very deflating and it made my life very difficsult for several years, but it was temporarily successful at moving me towards pursuing a "normal' life." I decided to get more involved with the joy and passion of my life by concentrating my efforts on my golf game. I was a 22 handicap back then and have steadily improved to a 6 handicap today. And I was even able to win the First Annual Senior King of the Hill Tournament in 2017 held at Eagle Point Golf Resort, shooting 76 Saturday and 73 Sunday.

Since then I have spent countless hours with my wife and golfing buddies racking up 2 holes in one with a goal to break 70 with 71 being my lowest score to date.

Since I was still feeling the weight of that court case, my tendency was to conduct my life in a more compliant relationship with the CRA and their presumptive authority.

But once you have taken the "Red Pill,"[1] you can never go back! Thus, a couple years after trying to lower my antenna and shutting down my senses, as well as recovering emotionally and mentally, my freedom loving spirit was drawn once again to other like-minded rebels.

---

[1] Red Pill from the movie The Matrix, once swallowed the participant leaves their illusory world and is awakened to true reality.

Chapter 2

YOU ARE A CORPORATION:
THE TRAP

*"The study of money, above all other fields in economics,
is one in which complexity is used to disguise or evade truth,
not to reveal it."*

~ *John Kenneth Galbraith* ~

Have you ever wondered why all of your legal documents have your name in all caps, from your birth certificate and passport to your drivers' license and medical records? Well, under the Roman Law of Capitis Deminutio your natural birthright lawful status is diminished to that of a legal taxable corporation.

This is their attempt at making the living beings into a corporation which is a dead entity and also note that all names on tombstones are always capitalized. The Universal Declaration of Human Rights lawfully states that all human beings are born free with their rights intact, but that all changes as soon as your parents sign your birth certificate which then makes you an artificial person and the legal property of the state.

I mentioned earlier where money is created from, that is, our birth certificate bonds. This is a complex process coveted mainly by the banking elite at the very top of the central banks of the world, primarily the BIS, IMF, World bank and The Federal Reserve.

A Birth Certificate is a negotiable instrument, a registered security, a stock certificate evidencing, or representing, the preferred stock of the corporation and against which you are the surety.

Everyone today is given a **CUSIP** number (**Committee on Uniform Security Identification Procedures**) which some experts even know how to look up on the stock exchange. The number can be found on your original Statement of Live Birth, if you can still get access to that. Usually they just give you a copy of the birth certificate, which is just a recording of the event.

The "ALL CAPS" name, sometimes referred to as "your strawman" is actually a trust which under trust law makes the state the trustee in control of your legal status and your parents the holder of the equitable benefits. But the legal status controlling your duties and obligations by the state far outweighs the beneficiary status held by your parents.

It was around 1933 when the Old Age Security was put in place. This was the ruling class throwing bread crumbs to the masses. It came into being in Canada about the same time, and most certainly with the same effect, requiring everyone to have a Social Insurance Number (SIN).

The ruling class had their people in the insurance industry at the time do an accrual evaluation of the potential lifetime earnings of the average citizen. It is in the millions today but was approximated at $640,000.00 back then. The figure is adjusted according to family history, and any promising character traits that may bolster the value of their stock such as famous athletes and movie stars.

Speaking of stocks, isn't it interesting to ponder how they used to bring their slaves to the "market" with hands and feet in "bonds," then once upon the platform floor they were held with their hands and heads in wooden "stocks." Here they were traded and sold on the original stock market floor.

Even before this time – actually it was in a 1913 quote from Edward Mandell House, advisor to President Woodrow Wilsdon, where he said. "[Very] soon, every American will be required to register their biological property in a national system designed to keep track of the people and that will operate under the ancient system of pledging. By such methodology, we can compel people to submit to our agenda, which will affect our security as a charge-back for our fiat paper currency. Every American will be forced to register or suffer being unable to work and earn a living. They will be our chattel, and we will hold the security interest over them forever, by operation of the law merchant under the scheme of secured transactions. Americans, by unknowingly or unwittingly delivering the bills of lading to us, will be rendered bankrupt and insolvent, forever to remain economic slaves through taxation, secured by their pledges. They will be stripped of their rights and given a commercial value designed to make us a profit and they will be none the wiser, for not one man in a million could ever figure our plans and, if by accident one or two should figure it out, we have in our arsenal plausible deniability. After all, this is the only logical way to fund government, by floating liens and debt to the registrants in the form of benefits and privileges. This will inevitably reap to us huge profits beyond our wildest expectations and leave every American a contributor to this fraud which we will call "Social Insurance." Without realizing it, every American will insure us for any loss we may incur, and in this manner every American will unknowingly be our servant, however begrudgingly. The people will become helpless and without any hope for their redemption, and we will employ the high office of the President of our dummy corporation to foment this plot against America."

We have also been made into corporations through legal statutes redefining the word person with a separation between "natural person" and "artificial person." You as a natural person have unwittingly given your permission and consent by application to and identifying with the all-caps name. Every time you fill out an application for everything from licenses to government certificates, be it medical forms or anything legal, the "ALL CAPS" name will be required.

Even the court proceedings have functions fashioned from ancient rituals and an example of their sorcery occurs when you receive a "summons" to court similar to a seance where a medium summons the dead. You are to "appear" in court, and they want you, the natural living person, to stand in for the dead "ALL CAPS" corporate name on the summons.

In any case, we are traded around the world like livestock or chattel in the trading markets by those in the know. So they make money on us from cradle to grave in this way, as well as through the many tax schemes, lending mechanisms, and derivatives. And let us not forget the inevitable inflation caused by this multi faceted and fraudulent fiat system.

All fiat money systems used by cultures from the Romans to the Chinese collapse after about 50 years because it becomes a mathematical impossibility to repay the compounded interest, never mind the principle.

In Canada we apply for a Social Insurance Number (SIN) to work and every other license or government service we apply for further confirms our obedience and subservience to that contract via our artificial all-caps name. If we look at the etymology of the word "government," simply put "govern" means to rule and "ment" is the mind. Thus it is mind control.

And most of us do not learn that upon reaching your 18th birthday you then become the beneficiary to the trust and could veritably begin to take control of your life by not applying for the SIN. The word sin means "to miss the mark" like an archer who cannot hit the bulls' eye and many versions of the Bible substitute the word debt for sin reading "forgive us our debts as we also have forgiven our debtors." They love to mess with scripture in all the religions where they vicariously instruct their subjects so as to "miss the mark."

Of course if you did not apply for the SIN you would find yourself unable to work under their system and would need to learn how to contract separately for work and most everything you embark on would take considerable effort and courage to accomplish. There are some who have gained their freedom this way, but it is definitely the road less traveled.

The creation of The Federal Reserve system[2] was a highly secretive meeting in one of the Elites 25 bedroom cottages on Jekyll Island off the coast of Georgia. It is a private corporation with its own jurisdiction much like the three cities London, the financial arm, Vatican City, the religious arm and Washington DC, the military industrial complex arm of the Globalist New World Order.

In the interest of the brevity of this work I will oversimplify how the three city states operate. The financial arm promotes itself by lobbying governments to borrow from its central bank and/or adopt democracy under threat of invasion from the military arm.

---

[2] The Creature From Jekyll Island by G. Edward Griffin,

The religious arm infiltrates countries under the guise of salvation for the people, and all the religions have been responsible for more torture and death than any other institution.

One of the back stories to the creation of the Fed is no coincidence and no accident and has been hidden in the sinking of the Titanic. The Titanic had a twin ship called The Olympic and was actually the one shipwrecked on that iceberg. Due to earlier accidents it was not insurable, so the night before departure the names were changed and while the Titanic sat in dry dock the Olympic set sail the next morning.

The date had been set for the meeting on the formation of The Federal Reserve Board at Jekyll Island, Georgia, but some of the wealthiest men in the world who were in opposition to the idea of a central bank never made it to that meeting. They had boarded the ship in hopes of quashing the vote. And at the last minute the owner of White Star Lines Shipping and one of the principles in the forming of the Federal Reserve System, J.P. Morgan, did not board, thus sealing the fate of those businessmen and ultimately ours.[3] I say ours because The Fed is connected to all the central banks and every country's currency is pegged to the US dollar.

There is no way I could have looked at any of this stuff while I was "in my cups." But I must say having experienced the cognitive dissonance phenomenon myself, I can empathize with those who are going through it now, but it takes a "red pill" experience to shake someone out of that spell.

I sobered up while working at Labatt Breweries in Toronto where I found myself in trouble over and over again until my supervisor Jim called me into the office to ask me to visit the plant doctor about my "drinking problem." I was enraged at the idea

---

[3] https://www.bitchute.com/video/Trm6Lk3XblcN/

because I knew deep down that alcohol was the only thing keeping me going, and without it, I would need to take a close look at me and what makes the world go round.

I am enjoying 40 years of sobriety today and I'm very grateful that Jimmy had the courage to confront me and get me enrolled in a 28 day 12 step program in Renaissance House.

Being "Red Pilled" can be very unsettling and traumatic when one realizes that long held belief systems of the so-called norm crumble under truisms that can no longer be denied. So the attraction to the illusive sovereign lifestyle continued to magnetize my pursuit of other avenues where I had heard and seen that some were having successes here and there. The problem was that after a few successes the powers that shouldn't be would close those doors and even make traps out of them, for which some found themselves heavily fined and or jailed.

That kind of news got around the movement and had the effect they desired of discouraging new anarchists from pursuing those techniques and reaping the same benefits.

A loosely knit group formed here in British Columbia and some of us stayed in contact, sharing information with each other as our research continued. We became aware of a retired Toronto lawyer who was very experienced in tax law, and he presented a Charitable Donation Program that offered a tax allowance. It was perfectly legal, and one could help people in 3rd world countries acquire generic drugs at a much lower price than the name brand prescriptions.

So I thought, "here is a humanitarian deed I can participate in while saving some money on taxes," and it looked like a win-win scenario. I felt very secure in the decision, and I found two other similar programs in the next couple years.

It was about 10 years later that the CRA decided to clamp down on all "charitable donation programs" so they retroactively changed the laws and were now disallowing the programs. I'm pretty sure it's illegal to change laws retroactively, and I am absolutely sure it is morally repugnant. Nevertheless the tax bullies were at it again tightening their economic stranglehold on all Canadians.

In the chart below one can see how government debt was coupled with the corresponding Canadian household debt.

It's all money magic operating on the High Seas with the use of words like "currencies" and "money flow." I spoke of the word "government" previously based on the Greek meaning "mind control" and now, complimenting that definition, we look at *Black's Law Dictionary 4th Edition.* The Latin word is gubernaculum which signifies the instrument, the helm, whereby the ship to which the state was compared, was guided on its course by the "gubernator" or helmsman.

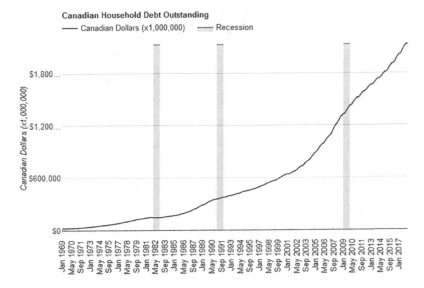

Source: Bank of Canada, Statistics Canada, Better Dwelling.

Look up Jordan Maxwell if you want to go deep on the subject of Merchant and Admiralty Law and how it is all performed on water. Starting at the breaking of mothers' water down the canal and arriving at the doc (tor) where it is berthed. If you do not claim your vessel at the age of 18 you are considered a ship lost at sea and the cargo of the state.

One of the most profitable schemes of all time was born out of an insurance fraud set up by Kings and Queens. Their ships laden with precious metals, expensive silks and spices would set sail for foreign ports with a very comprehensive insurance policy. The King would then hire pirates and pay a handsome commission for them to raid the bounty thus insuring the Kings' cargo and doubling his profits.

By the way, I'm sure most Americans are aware of the conspicuous imprint on the U.S. one dollar bill, that is the all-seeing eye of the god Horus at top of the pyramid. But of lesser notoriety are the words "*ANNUIT COEPTIS NOVUS ORDO SECLORUM*" Latin for *ANNOUNCING THE BIRTH OF THE NEW WORLD ORDER!* And its beginning is noted in the Roman numerals 1776. And how many are aware that the word "money" means "one eye"?

Take the federal reserve note created in 1913 when 100 cents was equal to one dollar, whereas now the value of that one dollar note is less than two cents. It's an illusion that prices keep going up when actually the value of the dollar is going down.

Take out a loan or a mortgage, which in the French language is mort (death) gage (pledge), a death pledge. They get the money from your birth bond, then have the audacity to lend you your own money at interest which triples the price and, in most cases, can take up to thirty years to pay for a house.

I realize how difficult this all can be to believe, especially if you happen to be in banking, but keep in mind, everything is on a need-to-know basis and your local bank manager is only taught procedures, not the mechanics of money creation. See *Hidden Secrets of Money* by Mike Maloney[4]

President Nixon canceled the fixed-rate convertibility of US dollars to gold in 1971 under orders from his bankster bosses. Their bank charter allows them to create nine times the original value of a loan with interest attached. And because the interest is not created, the debt becomes so great that this Fiat money mechanism ensures the mathematical impossibility to pay it all back. The monetary enslavement of entire governments occurs when they are required to collateralize their land and people to repay for wars financed on both sides by the international banksters.

Then, as in the planned 1929 economic collapse, when widespread bankruptcies take place in everything from small businesses to corporations and housing complexes, the ruling class buys up every property and business they want for pennies on the dollar.

I am reminded of the quote by John D. Rockefeller where he said, "Own nothing, control everything". And these banksters have their own definition of the "Golden Rule." "Whoever owns the gold makes the rules."

Another note of interest is that The FBI, Federal Reserve System, The Internal Revenue System and The Anti Defamation League were all created in 1913.

There are no coincidences, everything is planned in detail and patience is exercised in awaiting the correct timing to execute the plan. That is why the international banksters took over The Bank of Canada at the same time, and we are now 50 years out from those maneuvers.

---

[4] https://goldsilver.com/hidden-secrets/

Now with the global economic collapse imminent, what a perfect time to stage a pandemic. The strategy for closing down small businesses and destroying economies worldwide, is to shift the blame from the banksters, to a bioweapon, disguised as a so-called virus.

This is one of the main reasons for the emergence of the recent BRICS bank with the founding members Brazil, Russia, India, China, and South Africa already influencing world affairs. And countries like Iran and Argentina have filed their applications to join as of July 18, 2022, with Saudi Arabia, Turkey, and Egypt wanting to follow. They propose an independent, gold backed banking system not under the control of the Rothschild Khazarian Money Magic system currently failing miserably.

It always seems like a small victory when people like Vladimir Putin thumbs his nose at the Rothschild bankers and withdraws from that system, until we learn that it is just another Dragon family controlling a different faction.

You see, in a fiat money system, the dollar is backed only by the faith we place in that system, rather than backed by gold or some other valuable commodity. Whereas the BRICS Bank will be backed by gold, which is definitely a much better way to finance countries, but it remains to be seen if the world's people will benefit.

These banking families and their superiors have 100-year plans towards global domination, which encompasses every facet of our lives. For a comprehensive study get the book *Crisis by Design* by John Wolfe.

We need to develop a fair energy exchange system with an equitable outcome for all parties where the individual can access their birth bond for all their needs and then some. Or even better, we claim our sovereignty and learn how to manifest what we need and want, making these parasites obsolete.

The GLOBAL PEOPLES MONETARY SYSTEM[5] (GPMS) is a very good start to the awakening populations around the world to come together and make the old-world systems null and void. As the consciousness of the planet awakens, her people are aligning to be the change we desire. Soon we will reach critical mass and the wizard behind the screen will be revealed and the evil will be dissolved, making way for the Golden Age.

---

[5] https://gpms.world/

Chapter 3

SECRET SOCIETIES:
OCCULT CONSPIRACIES

"...in early times, it was easier to control a million people, literally it was easier to control a million people than physically to kill a million people. Today, it is infinitely easier to kill a million people than to control a million people. It is easier to kill than to control..."
Obama advisor ~Zbigniew Brzezinski ~

With that in mind, we have a look at the European faction of the family.

Rothschild's 25 Point Plan for World Domination

1. Use violence and terrorism rather than academic discussions.

2. Preach "Liberalism" to usurp political power.

3. Initiate class warfare.

4. Politicians must be cunning and deceptive – any moral code leaves a politician vulnerable.

5. Dismantle "existing forces of order and regulation." Reconstruct all existing institutions.

6. Remain invisible until the very moment when it has gained such strength that no cunning or force can undermine it.

7. Use Mob Psychology to control the masses. "Without absolute despotism one cannot rule efficiently."

8. Advocate the use of alcoholic liquors, drugs, moral corruption and all forms of vice, used systematically by "agenteurs" to corrupt the youth.

9. Seize properties by any means to secure submission and sovereignty.

10. Foment wars and control the peace conferences so that neither of the combatants gains territory placing them further in debt and therefore into our power.

11. Choose candidates for public office who will be "servile and obedient to our commands, so they may be readily used as pawns in our game."

12. Use the Press for propaganda to control all outlets of public information while remaining in the shadows, clear of blame.

13. Make the masses believe they have been the prey of criminals. Then restore order to appear as the saviors.

14. Create financial panics. Use hunger to control and subjugate the masses.

15. Infiltrate Freemasonry to take advantage of the Grand Orient Lodges to cloak the true nature of their work in philanthropy. Spread their atheistic-materialistic ideology amongst the "Goyim" (gentiles).

16. When the hour strikes for our sovereign lord of the entire World to be crowned, their influence will banish everything that might stand in his way.

17. Use systematic deception, high-sounding phrases and popular slogans. "The opposite of what has been promised can always be done afterwards… That is of no consequence."

18. A Reign of Terror is the most economical way to bring about speedy subjection.

19. Masquerade as political, financial and economic advisers to carry out our mandates with Diplomacy and without fear of exposing "the secret power behind national and international affairs."

20. Ultimate world government is the goal. It will be necessary to establish huge monopolies, so even the largest fortunes of the "Goyim" will depend on us to such an extent that they will go to the bottom together with the credit of their governments on the day after the great political smash."

21. Use economic warfare. Rob the "Goyim" of their landed properties and industries with a combination of high taxes and unfair competition.

22. "Make the 'Goyim' destroy each other so there will only be the proletariat left in the world with a few millionaires devoted to our cause, and sufficient police and soldiers to protect our interest."

23. Call it The New Order. Appoint a Dictator.

24. Fool, bemuse and corrupt the younger members of society by teaching them theories and principles we know to be false.

25. Twist national and international laws into a contradiction which first masks the law and afterwards hides it altogether. Substitute arbitration for law.

Who would possibly agree to this plan for world domination? To better understand who we are up against look at this statement.

"No one will enter the New World Order unless he or she will make a pledge to worship Lucifer. No one will enter the New Age unless he will take a Luciferian initiation." Director of Planetary Initiative United Nations ~ David Spangler

The United Nations is only one of their many tentacles that controls the various political systems around the world no matter whether liberal or conservative, fascist or communist, they control it all, playing one side against the other to divide and rule. Some others are The Council On Foreign Relations (CFR) and The Senior Executive Service (SES). Their pledges are moved around frequently between organizations, corporation boards, banks, and government to effectively control every aspect imaginable.

The business of governments and societies are far too important to the elite mafia's globalist agenda to allow their "chattel" to determine its direction and that includes the Mob.

And, I am continually amazed by the insight of Mark Twain who said "It is easier to fool someone than to tell them they have been fooled."

I tried to convince a former golfing buddy of mine that the JFK assassination was a joint CIA and government hit. He responded that he believed it was the Mafia, but I wasn't referring to who actually carried out the evil deed, I was more concerned with who gave the orders. "Lucky" Luciano controlled the shipping and unions on the east side docks even during his time in prison, but why was he released after serving 10 years of a 30-50 year prison sentence? The American government was concerned about wartime spies and German ships accessing the ports and so the plan known as Operation Underworld was born. Luciano guaranteed the protection of American ships based on the eastern seaboard that were vulnerable to German attack; in return for his wartime cooperation, he was released in 1946. Thus when known mafioso, Jack Ruby, carried out the assassination, it looked like it was revenge against the Kennedy brothers for their coordinated efforts to take down organized crime. But the lucrative International Drug trade made possible by the Vietnam War made up for the loss of their casino enterprise in Cuba, and the 100s of arrests on Luciano's prostitution ring by prosecutor Thomas Dewey.

Lyndon B. Johnson escalated that war but the international banksters were more concerned with stopping any further printing of the 4.3 billion in U.S. interest free notes that Kennedy ordered. Canceling those notes was Johnsons' first order of business while he was being sworn in on the plane trip to the oval office.

On June 4, 1963, an attempt was made to strip the Federal Reserve Bank of its power to loan money to the government at interest. On that day President John F. Kennedy signed Executive Order No. 11110 that returned to the U.S. government the power to issue currency to stimulate the economy. The last speech that President Kennedy gave sealed his fate when he stated, "For we are opposed around the world by a monolithic and ruthless conspiracy that relies primarily on covert means for expanding its sphere of influence, infiltration instead of invasion, subversion instead of elections, on intimidation instead of free choice, on gorillas by night instead of day."[6]

President Lincoln met the same fate for issuing "GreenBacks" interest free into the economy of his day. Many people are not aware that one of the primary reasons for the mass migration to the US and Canada from 1880's to 1920's was to escape the economic oppression in Europe by the King and his handlers, the Rothschilds. Mayer Amschell Rothschild proclaimed, " *Let me issue and control a nation's money and I care not who writes the laws.* " Then he sent his 5 sons into the European marketplace to set up their banks. Mayer and his eldest son, Amschel, supervised the growing

---

[6] https://www.bitchute.com/video/3aV3rmlR9Gim/

business from Frankfurt while Nathan established a branch in London in 1804. Jakob settled in Paris in 1811, and Salomon and Karl opened offices in Vienna and Naples, respectively, in the 1820s. They were successfully able to fund both sides of the Napoleonic and French revolutionary wars, a tactic the family still uses to this day, increasing their accumulated net worth which can only be estimated to be in the trillions, due to their many very well hidden offshore accounts.

Many Americans are still not aware that The Federal Reserve is not part of their government and that there are no reserves and it is not federal. The former chairman of the Fed, Alan Greenspan when interviewed by Jim Lehrer, stated "Well, first of all, the Federal Reserve is an independent agency, and that means, basically, that there is no other agency of government which can overrule actions that we take.

This quote by Thomas Jefferson says it all. "I believe that banking institutions are more dangerous to our liberties than standing armies. If the American people ever allow private banks to control the issue of their currency, first by inflation, then by deflation, the banks and corporations that will grow up around the banks will deprive the people of all property until their children wake up homeless on the continent their fathers conquered."

The Rockefeller oil cartel, in collusion with the corrupt Nixon Administration, managed to convince the leaders of the world that 1) oil (like gold) was a finite substance and that 2) all oil should be purchased in dollars only because the dollar was the world's reserve currency! This change allowed the oil and banking cartel the opportunity to control what the world would have to pay for a barrel of oil and allow them to inflate the dollar without restriction.

The status of the petrodollar is maintained by the US military, as both Saddam Hussein and Libya's Ghadafi found out when they attempted to sell their oil in Euros and Dinars backed by gold. It's the fastest way to become a terrorist! Just look at what has happened with Putin since he kicked the Rothschild bank out of Russia.

Much has been written and documented on money creation and its accompanying fraud. This is just an overview, so as not to get too depressing. We are more interested in solutions, and solutions that make the old-world systems obsolete.

There is a new player on the scene named Kimberly Ann Goguen, Ground Command and Guardian of the Global Assets.[7] She was in banking prior to being promoted to operate the Quantum Financial System, and I have been following Kim since about 2013 with considerable skepticism mixed with hope because her weekly updates are very revealing.

She has been perceived by many, including me, to be the one who will change the centralized banking system to a decentralized system for the benefit of humanity. She announced in one of her weekly broadcasts that the Cabal no longer have access to our Birth Bonds. She claims to operate the back end of the global financial system which formerly funded world governments and the militaries. Soon we will be able to access our own accounts for essential needs such as food, housing and medical care. But first we need to claim our sovereignty and draw up projects for the restoration of our planet and the healing of our people.

Many have already submitted business plans and executive summaries laying the foundation for such projects.

---

[7] https://www.unitednetwork.tv/

CHAPTER 4

THE PROPAGANDA ARMS:
EDUCATION AND MEDIA

*"If you don't read the newspaper you're uninformed, if you do
read the newspaper you're misinformed."*

~ *Mark Twain* ~

"We are grateful to the Washington Post, The New York Times, Time Magazine and other publications whose directors have attended our meetings and respected their promises of discretion for almost forty years. It would have been impossible for us to develop our plan for the world if we had been subject to the bright lights of publicity during those years. But the world is now more sophisticated and prepared to march toward a world government." At the private meeting of the Bilderberg

~ *David Rockefeller* ~

Remember grade school where we were taught how to read and spell? Well these educational systems are another form of control, infiltrated and funded by the oligarchs who use all kinds of black magic to cast their word spells to hypnotize the masses with their doctrine of deceit. The schools from kindergarten to the most prestigious universities are continually having their policies and textbooks updated with the latest propaganda to ensure the compliant capture of the developing generation.

Everything is by design, even the word school as in "school of fish" implies everyone doing something similar and going in the same direction. We spend our formative years learning to respect and obey authority–having been seated in uniform rows with our hands folded, we shut up and listen. Those 6 years are critical to our indoctrination with a belief system that promotes a lack of everything such as money, oil and food to name a few. This along with our secondary school training primes us to be constantly in survival mode accompanied by massive debt to facilitate the lifestyle of our desires. All based on lies!

Most of the Boards of Education and Universities are funded by enormous grants offered from the elite families and their foundations in each country who ensure their desired ideology and doctrine by infiltrating these institutions.

We are mesmerized by the phenomenon of cognitive dissonance. This phenomenon has recently become widespread due to the "Fear Porn" coming from the mainstream media and their "medical mafia" regarding the whole COVID 19 scamdemic.

In the 1940s and 50s there were advertisements, where the tobacco industry used doctors to promote smoking as beneficial. Just stop and think about the enormity of that lie and how many people died and/or had their health severely compromised as a result of believing the mainstream media of the time. You would think the regulatory bodies such as the FDA, Health Canada and the respective agencies in other jurisdictions would have caught Big Tobacco right at the beginning and made it illegal. But the profits made can and are well distributed to lobbyists and all the very well controlled political and media outlets.

Imagine the confidence and audacity that the former director of the CIA William Casey had to have in 1981 when he said, "We'll know our disinformation program is complete when everything the American public believes is false." Statements like these are not widely reported in the mainstream for obvious reasons.

One of the most knowledgeable people on the planet who was exposing corruption way back when it was very unpopular and dangerous to do so is David Icke. He is so much a threat to the well-being of the Deep State that on November 6, 2022 he was denied access to the Netherlands where he had a speaking engagement. If that wasn't enough the immigration order extended to 26 countries in the EU's passport-free Schengen travel zone.. Remember this whenever the mainstream labels someone a terrorist, it simply means he is terrifying to them and their agenda. Sign up for his newsletter at www.davidicke.com.

Sociopaths like Bill Gates, Tedros Adhanom Ghebreyesus, head of The World Health Organization (WHO), Klaus Schawb, head of the World Economic Forum (WEF), and many of the government appointed medical advisors in each country, are simply following the Rockefeller "Lock Step" program developed in 2009. It has been scrubbed from their website, so it is very difficult to find at present. Concerning Agenda 21 we are already in the 2nd generation of their 100 year plan to destroy society from within, whereas the details for Agenda 2030 are being rolled out in this decade.

These plans are facilitated by the bought and paid for mainstream media including the Hollywood Studios, radio and television. They are all scripted and controlled by their bosses. Even information sites like Wikipedia, YouTube and so called "Fact Checkers" have censors on the payroll in a desperate attempt to keep the truth on any given topic from surfacing.

They have some sort of loose moral code based on "informed consent" where they are required to tell us what they are doing before it is brought forth. Many times they warn us on their own websites or in movies, and it manifests as "predictive programming" but only if you know how they operate can you see it everywhere. The problem with that is that the "sheeple" believe most of their lies or are inwardly afraid of the changes in thinking and lifestyle they feel they would need to make. The search for truth requires critical thinking skills and the humility to change the mind when confronted with new information. Like Aristotle said, "Be a free thinker and don't accept everything you hear as truth. Be critical and evaluate what you believe in." Use inductive reasoning because it is the basis upon which all law rests and it consists of comparing a number of separate instances with each other until the common factor which gives rise to them all is seen.

A journalist asked a man on the street, "Do you think people are ignorant and apathetic?" The man replied, "I don't know, and I don't care!" Apathy is the desired state of mind that the Cabal produced by a never-ending barrage of one crisis after another. The intent is to confuse and demoralize us to the point we throw up our hands in exhaustion and surrender to their evil plans.

It is all by design and there is little time left to investigate and research after getting an education in the established 12-year indoctrination schools. It is a struggle just to earn a good living while keeping current with debt commitments.

Now, the question is, "what's the difference between a 'Conspiracy Theory' and the Truth?" And the answer is, "About 5 months."

In 2015 I attended Anarchapulco hosted by Jeff Berwick and his team where I was completely blown away by the quality and variety of speakers and subject matter. This was only their 2nd Annual Conference, and they were thrilled to have doubled attendance over the first year, and it did continue doubling attendance each year since, while expanding its many services and education. Jeff has announced that the 2023 Anarchapulco Conference will be limited to 1000 applicants due to the venue requirements. And I must say that this is real education with substantial knowledge of actual processes in alternative finance, home schooling, politics, medicine and every other topic under the sun.

Jeff does a very fun walk with his dogs Lucy and Lucky where he reveals nuggets of truth from his latest research here: https://rumble.com/v1jpmo9-ding-dong-the-reptiles-gone-long-live-climate-change-and-social-credit.html?mref=6zof&mc=dg-ip3&utm_source=newsletter&utm_medium=email&utm_campaign=DollarVigilante&ep=2

Jeff was talking about Bitcoin way back when it was 30 cents, then again at $3.00 but good ole cognitive dissonance kept me from looking at it until it went to $100.00 when I started further investigation. But, it was still too new and outside the box for me. Then someone said something that showed up in my inbox, that made me pay attention and jogged my memory, and it went something like this. "In the late 70s when the first personal computer came out, the mainstream media said that it would never go anywhere!" Again in the mid 90s when the internet came out, the mainstream media said, "that'll never go anywhere." It was about 2015 when I heard in the mainstream media that Bitcoin would never go anywhere, that's when I knew we were on to something because I had already learned a distrust for the media. I dipped my toes in the water around then quite modestly, and I am still eagerly anticipating what may be the final bull run. Although there is talk in some circles that the elite may not allow the currency exchanges a means for the retail public to liquidate their crypto. Unless we figure out a way to use it as an energy exchange between ourselves, we may get stuck holding it all at a loss. And of course with all the smoke and mirrors in the financial markets there are no guarantees, so when the bull runs, I will be taking profits.

One of the many fascinating speakers I met at Anarchapulco that year was "ken of the house of cousens" and he introduced me to his Gemstone University and PanTerra d' Oro. This is a massive storehouse of knowledge encompassing over 50 years of research and a private association which boasts of its own jurisdiction.

I added to my knowledge and began the process of setting up an Estate Structure with a view towards Status Correction which is the ultimate goal that they teach. As exciting as all that sounds, I found it overwhelming to the point that it seemed counterintuitive to my underlying belief that the awakening of humanity has more to do with the decalcification of the pineal gland and the upgrading of our DNA to move to a higher expression of being. And not so much the reverse engineering of the "mystery of iniquity" II Thessalonians 2:7, through a very complex process which enables those who can devote the time, energy and memorization to accomplish their freedom.

I'm not discounting the need for each of us to do our inner work to put the ego in place and allow our spiritual nature to flourish. I just wasn't prepared to spend all that time learning how to implement the complex process of correcting one's status, although I do agree we all need to have some awareness of these systems of enslavement. My focus in this book is more about bringing awareness of our adversaries and where to find solutions that will eventually make them obsolete. Many of their members are fully engaged at the highest level of participation in order to discover the concepts and technologies that will make that all possible. Ken and his wife Andrea are loving, caring, very compassionate and extremely patient people which I'm sure you will agree are characteristics to be admired and desired. And they both know it's not for everyone, but they are helping many freedom loving people with their courses. For those who would like to investigate, the site is here: https://www.gemstoneuniversity.org/master-plan.html.

You will find a wealth of knowledge on that site if you're so inclined–everything from natural health remedies, alternative energy solutions, to projects for the benefit of mankind which offer solutions to most of the world's problems.

Now, the after round musings in the clubhouse is not the best place to divulge information like you are finding here, as I have learned over the years. It's just that I am pretty much an open book and probably should have more of a filter on my conversation, and I am working on it, simply trying to discern when and who to open up to because most people do not want to broach the uncomfortable.

Klaus Schwab the founder of the WEF has bragged that more than half of Crime Minister Trudeaus' cabinet in Ottawa comprises his Young Leaders program. If you take the time to investigate and have a close look at the "nice sounding" policies on the WEF website, it reveals their communist, fascist roots. Notice a lot of these medical advisors in Canada are administrators and have had limited to zero experience in the actual treatment of patients. People like Teresa Tam, Chief Medical Officer for Canada, and Bonnie Henry, Health Officer for the Province of BC, who were trained in the Young Leaders program at the WEF have no loyalty to Canadians, only their foreign masters.

Trudeau himself has admired the Chinese Communist Party, citing how their "dictatorship has turned their economy around on a dime." Chinese police stations have sprouted up recently in New York, USA and Toronto, Canada partly because these cities have a large Chinese population. Media reports state "Due to the COVID-19 epidemic, many overseas Chinese citizens are not able to return to China in time for their Chinese driver's license renewal and other services." Many local Chinese fear that it is a way for the officials to silence dissidents and threaten their families back home.

Although Trudeau would very much love to be the dictator of Canada, it is mainly the top corporations controlling our governments. Call it corporatocracy or technocracy. They are preferring this type of government over the popular propaganda that we have named a democracy.

Many of our politicians have contracts for things like the plexiglass dividers and yellow and red floor directional arrows to keep the cattle moving in accordance with the guidelines. After all, there were more billionaires made during Covid than any other time, and the existing billionaires increased their wealth 20-fold, according to Gates himself.

Peaceful United Non-Compliance is how we overcome the tyranny we are experiencing!

People are paralyzed by the constant bombardment of fear tactics resulting in a disabling of their critical thinking skills and closing them off to reason. With their heads in the sand, they refuse to take a look at the research by countless medical professionals who have written hundreds of peer reviewed papers.[8] As previously discussed, Cognitive dissonance is a type of hypnosis that can be, and is, purposefully developed in populations through many mediums of scripted education and media.

This is all reinforced by telling us that we have overpopulated the earth and are the cause of all the poverty, pollution and climate change, so we need to reduce the world population through abortion and vaccines.

In a Ted Talk, Bill Gates (of Hell) exposes himself again with his formula for population reduction:

P = People, S = Services per person, E = Energy per service, C = CO_2 per energy unit

Then he adds that in order to get CO_2 to zero, "probably one of these numbers is going to have to get pretty close to zero."

Following that, Gates begins to describe how the first number – P (for People) – might be reduced. He says: "The world today has 6.8 billion people… that's headed up to about 9 billion. Now if we do a really great job on *new vaccines, health care, and reproductive health services*, we could lower that by perhaps 10 or 15 percent."

Say what? "If we do a really great job on new vaccines…

How about that he isn't hiding it anymore. Oh yeah! And this is the computer geek with a business plan where he creates an operating system, which pays handsomely, but leaves "back doors" in it for a "virus attack" so he can then create an antivirus program to further increase his profits. Definitely not a team player in favor of the restoration of our planet and her people.

---

[8] Dr. Peter McCullough https://www.uscjournal.com/authors/peter-mccullough

The Johns Hopkins Center for Health Security in partnership with the World Economic Forum and the Bill and Melinda Gates Foundation hosted Event 201, a high-level pandemic exercise on October 18, 2019, in New York, NY. The exercise illustrated areas where public/private partnerships will be necessary during the response to a severe pandemic in order to diminish large-scale economic and societal consequences.

Gates and his co-conspirators held Event 201 under the following guise from their website.

To be clear, the Center for Health Security and partners did not make a prediction during our tabletop exercise. For the scenario, we modeled a fictional coronavirus pandemic, but we explicitly stated that it was not a prediction. Instead, the exercise served to highlight preparedness and response challenges that would likely arise in a very severe pandemic. We are not now predicting that the nCoV-2019 outbreak will kill 65 million people.

Yeah sure! They are not predicting, but they certainly are working towards it, and all this talk about the overcrowding of the planet and the need to reduce the population is a big crock of elitist dung.

There is enough land for everyone on planet earth to fit into the state of Texas[9] and of course no one wants to do that, but we can see how ridiculous their claim of depopulation is by looking at the example below.

The occupancy of humanity, living in groups of four within 1,000 square-foot households, is 25.71% of the square footage of Texas. The world population is approaching 8 billion but as of April 2019, the estimated human population is 7.7 billion and the square footage of Texas is 7,487,603,500,000 square feet at approximately 1000 sq.ft. per person.

---

[9] https://www.pop.org/episode-1-overpopulation-the-making-of-a-myth/

Here is that math:

If, on average, all of humanity were living in groups of four (7.7 billion / 4 = 1,925,000,000), there would be 1,925,000,000 (1.9 billion) households.

If these households were 1,000 square feet each (1.925 billion x 1,000), households would occupy 1,925,000,000,000 (1.925 trillion) square feet.

Compare this number (1.925 trillion sq ft) to the square footage of Texas (7.488 trillion sq ft).

The brazen arrogance of these people becomes more and more in our faces as each year passes. They believe they have untouchable power that allows them to say and do anything they want. It reminds me of a narcissist who I had a conversation with a few years ago when I confronted him with the errors of his ways, and his response to me was, "Even when I'm wrong, I'm right!" I couldn't process it then, but it gave me insight into the mindset of these people and the necessity to disassociate.

They use black magic and spells to conjure up the desired outcome in their target audience. Even the very word "spelling" is no accident in language. Much of the language employs short phrases which are continually repeated over and over again such as "be safe" and "we are all in this together" or "keep 6 feet apart."

"If you tell a lie big enough and keep repeating it, people will eventually come to believe it. The lie can be maintained only for such a time as the State can shield the people from the political, economic and/or military consequences of the lie. It thus becomes vitally important for the State to use all of its powers to repress dissent, for the truth is the mortal enemy of the lie, and thus by extension, the truth is the greatest enemy of the State." ~ Joseph Goebbels

They bought and paid for the media to push the stories that bolster their various agendas. Take for instance how they set up organizations and lobbies with ubiquitous funding to discredit the entire holistic medicine movement. They make them out to be quacks practicing pseudoscience when in reality their patients have experienced countless benefits in their health.

So we now have the darkside scrambling ever since that solstice in 2012, trying to cover their tracks and scurrying about like rats trapped in a cage, as they are being more and more exposed. The most terrifying of all their deeds revealed is their main control mechanism, which is the rampant and far-reaching pedophile network that spans every continent and every country. The level of infiltration permeates Hollywood and the political landscape where the most influential of their servants can operate up until now undetected with impunity but only given to those who do the bidding of the master. Not everyone succumbs to their wishes though! Take Mel Gibson who has risked everything by making statements like this, "Hollywood is an institutionalized pedophilia ring. It is a den of parasites who feast on the blood of children. Every studio in Hollywood is bought and paid for with the blood of children."

It begs the question why would anyone cooperate? But a lot of it is on a "need to know" basis where the participants just believe they are making a scary movie. The insiders who are well aware and willingly playing their parts are sold out initiates and very much into the Luciferian religion. Then there are those who are bribed, not only with enormous pay cheques, but also through many years of involvement in pedophilia. Many actors, producers and directors were brought up in these luciferian families from birth and groomed via ritual abuse, torture and mind control.

Adrenochrome is a highly addictive drug drawn from the adrenal gland at the time when fear is heightened through terror during these rituals which are conjured up mainly at specific times of year like the different solstices and holidays (holydays) such as Easter and Halloween.

Consider the Babylon Mystery Religion[10] where the ancient Sun Goddess of fertility in Phoenicia was known as Astarte (Easter). The Egyptian Goddess of fertility, (eggs and bunny rabbits) was Isis, and at Ephesus she was known as Diana, and every culture had their own Queen of Heaven with a different name but the same practice. The legend was that Nimrod the King of Babylon, after his death, was resurrected and lay with his Goddess virgin wife Semiramis during the spring solstice of Easter. Nine months later at the December winter solstice, she gave birth to the Sun god Tammuz. Pagan religions practiced these two feast days long before the 1st century. It wasn't until The Council of Nicea in 325 CE that the Roman Emperor Constantine made it law. He was well aware of the rapidly increasing numbers of the sect known as the Essenes. They were practicing Christ consciousness and were threatened with adopting these Holy days or being thrown to the lions.

Note also the evolution of media psychology with the passing of time, and each new decade becomes more violence, more blood, more demoralization. This all facilitated the breakdown of the family structure and the basic values and principles that guided us in the formulation of our societies. Simple things like the art of conversation have suffered greatly as we go out for dinner or sit in a bar and watch people at tables fully engaged with their cell phones and only partially engaged with their friends and family around the dinner table.

---

[10] Babylon Mystery Religion Ralph Woodrow, 1981

I touched on how they capture the youth by means of parental compliance and through government agencies such as Child and Family Services and then there is the smuggling through underground tunnels and the clandestine cross border child trafficking.

Many of these deviant occult practices go back for centuries, and recently some of their symbols were exposed by the FBI.

Intellectual activist and poet Sacha Stone was instrumental in establishing The International Tribunal for Natural Justice *ITNJ Treaty* on the 14th of February 2015, in memory of St. Valentine who died defending the natural rights of the people on that day 1700 years ago. I am proud to be one of the many people who ratified the Proclamation and in receipt of said document autographed by Sacha himself. You can find Sachas' podcast at http:// ariseguerrillanews.com/live/

(U) BLogo aka "Boy Lover"

(U) LBLogo aka "Little Boy Lover"

(U) GLogo a.k.a. "Girl Lover," Childlove

(U) CLogo a.k.a. "Chi Lover"

The FBI released symbols which represent sexual preferences for children

Note the "Boy Lover" logo on the Pope's robe.

It is believed that adrenochrome is some sort of elixir to keep a youthful appearance and therefore very much in demand. And apparently the harvested adrenochrome is more addictive than heroin.

The Bible is replete with child and blood sacrifice to the gods, and the ancient religion flourishes today as these terrifying family traditions are passed down. They have been discovered everywhere from monarchies to politics and Hollywood because their lust for power has blinded them; it has been reported that symbology will be their downfall.

Many good people go into politics with a mind to make positive changes for the benefit of their community, but if they rise to a position of influence they must be controlled. First bribery attempts are made, then if the moral compass of the victim does not succumb to offers of a huge bank account and initiation into the club, they set a "Honey trap." In this trap the victim is lured in using alcohol and/ or drugs and beautiful young women that are captured on video or photographed in compromising positions. Now that's a life-changing moment that is used to blackmail and control the candidate if necessary, but many go willingly into the dark night of the soul for the pure lust for power and enormous wealth. This is what we have been dealing with for centuries and this quote from Henry Kissinger explains their mindset. "Who controls the food supply controls the people; who controls the energy can control whole continents; who controls money can control the world." He also said, "The illegal we do immediately. The Unconstitutional takes a little longer".

Chapter 5

KHAZARIAN DECEIT:
THE ENEMY WITHIN

"I do not like the reappearance of the Jesuits... Shall we not have regular swarms of them here, in as many disguises as only a king of the gypsies can assume, dressed as printers, publishers, writers and schoolmasters? If ever there was a body of men who merited damnation on earth and in Hell, it is this society of Loyola's. Nevertheless, we are compelled by our system of religious toleration to offer them an asylum."

~ John Adams, letter to Thomas Jefferson, May 5, 1816 ~

One clear sign that the Globalists are running scared is the recent proclamation by the United Nations that it has declared war on "Conspiracy Theories". Under the proclamation of their latest war, they basically tell us what to think and how to say it in a politically correct manner. They describe the rise of conspiracy thinking as "worrying and dangerous," and provide the public with a toolkit to "prebunk" and "debunk" anybody who dares to suggest that world governments are anything but completely honest, upstanding and transparent. They are scrambling to discredit everything that runs counter to the narrative, like a kid laying on the floor kicking and screaming because she was denied her candy. And one of the biggest babies in the world is Canadian "Crime Minister" Justin Castro Trudeau tabling his ass kissing censorship Bill C-11 where we won't even have a choice because algorithms will decide what we can and cannot see. There is just one problem with the UN's definition of a "real" conspiracy theory. The media has been fully bought and paid for by the elite. It is the deep state who are conspiring against the masses as shown when Trudeau first funded the CBC in Canada where he stated further funding would depend on "if they cooperate".

The CIA coined the term "conspiracy theory" after the assassination of JFK in order to shut down the alternate views of how it all took place. Anything that runs counter to the mainstream medias' narrative since then, is quickly tagged with that misnomer. It is very effective in keeping people from investigating or even daring to take a peek at another point of view. You know you are getting close to the truth when they start censoring anything you say in a post, watch in a video or read; it's the best way to know that you have struck a nerve that they do not want exposed. It is almost a guarantee that anything the three letter agencies are accusing someone of is exactly what they are doing themselves. Things like the wiretapping of US citizens which is against CIA code.

Abraham Lincoln said, "America will never be destroyed from the outside. If we lose our freedoms, it will be because we have destroyed ourselves from within."

You would think that if these "conspiracy theories" were espoused by "tin foil hat" wearing unpatriotic derelicts in their basements, they would have nothing to worry about. But when these theories are fleshed out with credible sources, they make a lot more sense than the narrative being spewed forth simultaneously in unison by the controlled media. Not to mention how so much of what goes on in the world defies logic and is completely counter to healthy life and actually promotes everything that causes sickness and death.

First they divide, creating classes that favor one over the other. Then there is the racial card used to foment attitudes, and there is of course the religious separation.

But they have no problem bringing these divided people together as troops, under the guise of patriotism, when their blood lust requires a sacrificial war to cull the populations, according to their eugenics plans.

Some will remember when George H. Walker Bush became the Director of the CIA on January 30, 1976, and in only one short year in the position he was able to improve relations between the Agency and Capitol Hill and repair that relationship by expanding the role of Congress in overseeing the CIA. This all brought him accolades while he insisted upon direct access to President Ford. He usually edited the President's Daily Brief, or briefed at National Security Council meetings, in order to convey CIA's analysis directly to the President. This put him in the very influential position to steer the country for the cabal and he said, *"I think we should think of the CIA as a national asset that must be preserved as a vital part of our defense system... It is important that the American people understand the intricate job the CIA is doing in an increasingly complex world. It is essential we have the support of the American people."*

George Bush senior is believed to have been behind the false flag operation known as 911. He was a master of propaganda like his Father Prescott Bush who is believed to have helped fund Hitler in WWII. And George was given a dishonorable and traitor's funeral shown by the wrinkled flag over his coffin.

Fear is one of their main weapons of control as it prevents our manifesting of our birthright. And it was Hemann Goering, when asked at the Nuremberg trial in1945. "How did you convince the German people to accept all this?" He said, "It was easy and has nothing to do with Nazism. The only thing a government needs to turn its people into slaves is fear, if you can find something to scare them you can make them do anything you want."

The United States Central Intelligence Agency (CIA) was created on September 18, 1947, when Harry S. Truman signed the National Security Act of 1947 into law. It is believed that many of Hitler's SS were secreted into the CIA under Bush's direction while Hitler himself, the great grandson of Nathan Rothschild, was secreted away to Argentina, and his clone was buried in Germany. Even here in Canada as many as 2,000 members of 14th SS Division Galicia arrived in Canada in the 1950s and immediately started to whitewash and cover up their past. Flight Lt. Bohdan Panchuk of The Royal Canadian Air Force managed to convince the Canadian government to accept these members of Adolf Hitler's Waffen SS.

It's hard to imagine and many will not believe that our governments and regulatory agencies would allow this to occur, but as we delve into the eugenics agendas promoted by the ruling elite it will become more clear. Let's take a look at how these families and their societies control corporations and manipulate the masses.

The Protocols of the Elders of Sion states how they use encrypted intelligence along with disseminated counterintelligence to achieve their goals in the continued acquisition of power and wealth.[11] This is the tactic that the Khazarian Mafia has used to confuse the masses to the point where formulating any kind of opinion seems futile. Political landscapes are captivated on all sides through infiltration and deceptive practices, in order to divide people on every position and keep us busy with the many topics of the day. This sets the necessary stage to carry out their evil agendas underground. The technique is referred to as The Hegelian Directive which is basically, Problem, Reaction, Solution. When populations react out of fear, the thinking is very unclear and desperate for a satisfactory response, so they are much more malleable and susceptible to whatever the mainstream narrative proposes as a solution. People develop an attitude of acceptance, but it is rooted in cognitive dissonance, and this modus operandi has been in play for centuries. It is repeated over again gradually with every change they make, like boiling a frog in what starts out as a nice warm place and literally ends in death. So as more rights are eroded and more acceptance of otherwise ludicrous events take place, they bring us into compliance. And it's all based in lies, deception and fraud and their pre-planned agenda is the solution, and with this in mind they carefully craft situations and events which instill fear, guilt and anger in the various populations around the world. Keeping humanity at a very low vibration, the technique has proven very beneficial to these occult masters and their puppeted politicians, orchestrating all kinds of nefarious deeds to tax and oppress the captured.

And social media type Mel K who said: " The Globalists' intent is not only to collapse the global financial system, the energy sys-

---

[11] Healing Codes of the Biological Apocalypse, pg. 125, 1999, Dr. Leonard Horowitz

tem and the supply chains and to commit genocide, they intend to collapse all the world's governments and to replace them with an artificial intelligence-driven system that ties your identity to a Central Bank Currency with track-and-trace technology, controlling where you can go and what you can buy. It is a Corporatist Fascist model that intends to side step government entirely."

Her website is themelkshow.com

The Khazarians would ride into towns and villages killing the men, and taking the women and children to rape, terrorize and use as slaves. But as time went on these techniques needed to be refined as civilizations grew up around the world. Then there are the advancements in technologies which they kept a very tight lid on by black listing new inventions at the patent offices. As well as pay offs and even killing the inventors, who cannot be bought out. Why and how could people possibly inflict this much pain, torture and suffering on anyone else? Only someone demonically possessed is capable of such atrocious acts of inhumanity, but to give you an idea of the mindset read the following quote from John D. Rockefeller.

"We will keep their lives short and their minds weak while pretending to do the opposite. We will use our knowledge of science and technology in subtle ways so that they never see what is happening. We will use soft metals, aging accelerators and sedatives in food and water as well as in the air. They will be covered in poisons wherever they turn. The soft metals will make them lose their minds. We will promise to find a cure from our many funds, and yet we will give them more poison. Chemical poisons will be absorbed through the skin of idiots who believe that certain hygiene and beauty products presented by great actors and musicians, will bring eternal youth to their faces and bodies, and through their thirsty and hungry mouths, we will destroy their minds and systems of internal organs. However, their children will be born as disabled and deformed and we will hide this information."

An extremely effective technique to muddy the waters and make it very difficult to discern the truth on any given operation began centuries ago by the aforementioned Khazarian Mafia,[12] a people more closely related to the Hun, Uigur and Magyar tribes of Eastern Europe. Their Empire was formed just north of the Black Sea in the southern section of Russia below Moscow. Prior to that time Josephus wrote how the Idumeans of Esau "became Jews" when they adopted the Jewish religion for political purposes. These children of Edom are still in world Jewry today.

After taking over a village or town by raids where they killed the men and raped the women and children and made them serve as slaves, they were then able to hide their true identities and character to any future visitors under the guise of presenting themselves as the rulers of the towns they overtook. When travelers were passing through, they would invite them to rest up for their ensuing journey and offer food, drink, lodging and whatever festivities they had planned that evening. Sometime during the night, usually after much merry making and drink, they would kill the unsuspecting nomad, then steal his identity, enabling them to then go on to commit all kinds of crimes.

This very stealthy manner of operating allows for infiltration into any kind of position of power and once in, the doors are opened for their cohorts to join them. The ultimate identity ruse was the conversion to a type of Jewish faith based in the Babylonian Talmud or the Satanic Egyptian Kabbalah, in which many

---

[12] https://politicalvelcraft.org/2018/12/27/the-hidden-history-of-the-rothschild-khazarian-mafia/

of Hollywood's famous are known to have made it their practice. Their origins have been traced to Eastern Europe between the seventh and tenth centuries C.E. where the impact of these religious imposters was widely felt throughout that area and brought about the racial and extensive hatred of the "Jews." DNA research from Dr. Eran Elhaik and associates at the McKusick-Nathans Institute of Genetic Medicine, Johns Hopkins University School of Medicine, have confirmed that 97% of the 17 million of the world's Jews ARE NOT descendants of Abraham.[13] There is a very telling 60 minutes interview of George Soros where Steve Kroft asks him if it was difficult confiscating property from the Jews in Nazi Germany. He says, "Not at all." Of course not because they are not his people!

The falsely acquired power of these imposters dates back to the beginning of man. Their tactic of mixing truth with deception shows up in the Bible at Revelation 2:9 where they actually blow the whistle on themselves about their true nature, "I know the blasphemy of them which say they are Jews, and are not, but are the synagogue of Satan."

The tactic is consistently used in the mediums of print and film as their preferred method of subterfuge for the brainwashing of the masses.

The former Satanist and hard-hitting Mark Passio reveals a ton of must-see information in his video on Natural Law[14] where he explains a scene from one of my favorite movies, The Matrix.

Very often it is the villain of the movie who reveals the truth as found in The Matrix. The evil Merovingian who refers to himself as "a trafficker of information," and I paraphrase, "You are coming to me without an understanding of why you are in this position. You don't

---

[13] https://theserapeum.com/the-jewish-paradox-imposter-hebrews/

[14] https://www.whatonearthishappening.com

understand the causal factors that led to your current conditions. You have no power to affect change. Why is the only source of real power. Without why you are powerless, causality is the only real truth."

Morpheus replies with the truth, "Everything starts with choice." Then the villain shows his true colors by countering with a falsehood "Free will is like an illusion."

We do have free will because our choices determine our reality. If our thoughts align with our words and produce actions that are in harmony with Natural Law, then the causality will affect the desired reality. Our difficulty becomes evident when habits, that were subconsciously formed in our first 7 years, persist in playing an undesired program that is not aligned with Natural Law. We beat ourselves up due to the frustration we feel when it seems futile to overcome.

The Khazarians have done everything in their power to keep us from learning Natural law, keeping us entertained and filling our lives with so much business to distract us from the truth.

Again Natural Law demands we think, feel and act in concert in order to connect with Unity Consciousness

The fundamental faith of the true "Jewish" people, the descendants of Abraham, Isaac, and Jacob, is rooted in the Torah, and the 1973 Jewish Encyclopedia documents that approximately 90% of the world's so-called Jews are Khazarian. These pseudo-Jewish are criminals who have adopted a type of Jewish faith, but rather than the Torah they based their faith in the Talmud which is full of black magic spells, witchcraft and satanic sorcery. Many of these identity thieves realized they would need to be in international banking to carry out the plan of world domination because centralizing institutions is key to population control.

Similar tactics with much more sophistication are used today by the several organizations that control much of the world today. The Society of Jesus run by the Jesuits is one such occult operation whereby the initiates take a blood oath to obey the commands of The General who may even instruct the disciple to kill himself if warranted. They may be instructed to pretend to adopt another faith, any faith, any political party, any occupation. They are also adept at acquiring positions on city councils, legal firms, boards of education. They weasel their way onto corporate boards of hospitals, banking, insurance industries and politics where they can influence important decisions that further the agendas of their masters. This extensive infiltration allows them to incubate their plans and eventually take over and dominate these systems, all of which has been going on for decades. Their pretenses extend to all fields of endeavor and particularly to governments from which the control mechanisms can ultimately extend right down to the individual.

Remember earlier the Rothschild's Point 11: The voting system is rigged so their people get in while the masses are under the illusion that they are participating in a represented democracy. And, like any other corporation, the top people in the organization are previously selected, not elected in by the public.

Notice how when a country's political party changes from a conservative to a liberal one that everything still moves along very much the same with only minor differences being volleyed about sustaining the status quo illusion.

It was Mark Twain who said, *"If voting made any difference, they wouldn't let us do it."*

Then there are many other organizations that are intertwined because of alliances made between key players who facilitate the passing of information, critical to clandestine operations. One of which is the alignment of The Jesuit General while in control of the Scottish Rite Freemasons with Adam Weisshaupt who founded the Illuminati 1776.

These groups are in the background but are the overlords pulling the strings and are referred to as The Illuminati, or more recently the Cabal or Deep State.

Freemason Lodges at the lowest levels are made up of good members of their respective business communities who organize social and charitable events that help raise money that benefit their towns and cities. Yes, this is true at the lower apprentice levels and on through guilds to Journeyman and so on where those members believe the G in the middle of their square and compass symbol stands for God, Geometry or The Great Architect of the Universe.

It is not until one has been groomed to the highest 33rd degree Mason that they learn the ultimate meaning of the G to be The Generative Principle or Genesis taught in esoteric Freemasonry. This creative principle is where they learn about the true nature of cause and effect, that where we focus our time and attention will manifest our experience. It is so simple that it is missed by most of us, me included, because we prefer to describe our prison rather than do the difficult inner work necessary to manifest our sovereign freedom.

Chapter 6

AWAKENING:
THE ONE HUNDREDTH MONKEY

*"Invention is the most important product of man's creative brain.
The ultimate purpose is the complete mastery of mind over the
material world, the harnessing of human nature to human needs."*

~ *Nikola Tesla* ~

The Unified Field, is an all-encompassing electromagnetic conscious energy that everyone and everything is a part of and interacting with, therefore it behooves us to learn how to cooperate with it as we move into the Age of Aquarius. We fasten our seatbelts and ready ourselves with enthusiastic expectations on this runway to a new era. Aquarius is known as the water bearer, where information becomes available to the collective consciousness via downloads into our being as well as multiple networks of sharing platforms being developed, similar to facebook, but without the censorship.

Ten strands of our DNA were unplugged but now we reconnect to fully functional 12 strands along with the decalcifying of our Pineal Gland. There is no such thing as "Junk DNA" that we were led to believe; our creator does not make junk. Chemicals like fluoride, herbicides and pesticides that we have been ingesting for decades, and more recently chemtrails and GMOs, were all designed to keep us "dumbed down" and unaware of our true potential.

Time has come for an awakening of the Christ Consciousness within, like he referred to in the Bible, that the works that he did, we also would do, and greater than these we would do.

Of course there is a mass awakening taking place at this time and we are hoping the "100th monkey effect" will soon manifest.

The hundredth monkey effect is a hypothetical phenomenon in which a new behavior or idea is spread rapidly by unexplained means from one group to all related groups once a critical number of members of one group exhibit the new behavior or acknowledge the new idea. The behavior was said to propagate even to groups that are physically separated and have no apparent means of communicating with each other.[15]

British in Hebrew means Brit (covenant) and ish (man). Many believe the migration of the 12 Tribes of Judah included the British Isles of England, Ireland, Scotland, and Wales, whereas other Tribes like Dan may have ended up in Denmark and so on. It is even believed that the Phoenicians were descended from Noah and were therefore the great shipbuilders of that era traveling even to North America long before Christopher Columbus. Some evidence for this comes from copper mines in the Canadian Province of Ontario that had been completely depleted and then this same ore was found in Soloman's Temple.

Many Christians believe we are now in the "End times" and Christians in times past also believed they were in the End Times.

---

[15] https://en.wikipedia.org/wiki/Hundredth_monkey_effect

We are actually in a transition from the end of the age of pisces and the beginning of the age of aquarius. The return of Christ will not be a physical savior but rather it is a returning "Christ Consciousness" that is awakening in humanity. That along with the revealing of a multitude of clean climate devices and inventions will also present us with an upgrade to 12 strands of DNA and an increasing vibratory rate toward the 5th dimension. Our increased vibration and frequency allows for mental telepathy communication and extra sensory abilities discussed extensively by Ismael Perez in his bestselling book, Our Cosmic Origins.

Remember back in 2012 when all the buzz in the mainstream media ridiculed the biblical and Mayan prophecies saying the world was going to end, then the winter solstice came and went on December 21-23 and they reported that "see, nothing happened". Yeah, nothing they were allowed to report on!

There is astronomical proof that during that solstice, Alcion, the superNova or Sun that our solar system revolves around, had lined up with our sun and our earth causing a massive infusion of light. Thus we entered the age of Aquarius and what had ended was the age of Pisces, and the end of the two fishes Mitre worn by the Pope signifying Dagon the fish God. The age of religion, superstition and darkness ended, not the end of our world. See figure below.

Interesting to note the mistranslation of the Greek word age (aion) 2 Corinthians 4.4 in the bible where it states, "the god of this (world) hath blinded the minds of them which believe not," should be the god of this (age). Or Mathew 13:39, "the harvest is the end of the world." Where the word (end) is syntelia in Greek meaning completion. Thus it is the completion of an age ruled by the Luciferian cult who worship Satan by their own admission.

This awakening is what truly scares the Khazarian Mafia because they know when this becomes apparent to a critical mass of humans, they will no longer have the ability to maintain the illusion of power and will become obsolete.

Our 3rd dimensional reality has already been upgraded to the 4th dimension for many truth seekers who now are thinking in that dimension and on that level. Some of the necessary requirements for 5th dimensional beings are a basic capacity for compassion and love. You may know that narcissists and sociopaths are incapable of these emotions.

Spiritual scientist Dr. Bruce Lipton and his fascinating work on epigenetics has shown that we are not our bodies, and he has shown how our consciousness can be measured being broadcast into us from outside our body. The rewriting of the history books coupled with media promotion is just one of the many techniques used by these wizards, and oh yes, my Christian friends, even the bible has not been protected by God as we were led to think. It is these deviant tyrants who say in their own literature that they worship Lucifer, Satan, Moloch and a host of many other names depending on the culture.

In the 1980's I was attracted to the Christian religion but not in the traditional churchgoing sense which never had any appeal for me. What we had was a Biblical research ministry rooted in Hebrew and Greek and studied in homes as was commonplace in the 1st century.

These early disciples were known as Essenes and understood the body of Christ to be a spiritual entity made up of people, not bricks and stained glass. Our cult-like organization had its faults much like many others, but we didn't care because we thought we knew the "Truth" and we were operating very close to the original God-breathed Word. Of course that's what most Christian sects believe, and with over 2000 different denominations you end up picking one based on a buffet style around convenience and your own formative experiences. Not to be too critical because I have great admiration for the millions of wonderful people trying to find where they fit in and how they can contribute to the benefit of all.

But if the Cabal infiltrated every facet of our lives, why would they leave this trillion-dollar industry and most profound area of belief to chance? Religion is at the core of control, divide and conquer, and the ultimate fear of death and possibility of eternal damnation for humans are major mechanisms for manipulation of entire populations. This presented the most difficult and emotionally charged transition of all for me and still has troubling aspects to it because some of my dear friends are Christians. Upon broaching the subject it becomes clear that they think I am a part of those who are falling away in the end times and still in need of salvation.

It wasn't until our home study group got into Church history and the development of doctrine over the centuries that we realized that our beloved Word of God had also been corrupted. Some of the other texts we looked at were The Dead Sea Scrolls, The Nag Hammadi and Summerian Texts. I am not pretending to have read them through, but I have read every word of the bible from cover to cover 4 times in addition to countless hours of study. For an excellent resource for all of this and much more see Billy Carson https://rumble.com/v1pqdyn-by-request-billy-carson-the-power-of-dna... enjoy.html

It was relatively easy to see how the Cabal had infiltrated banking, governments, medicine, science, media, education and basically every facet of our lives, but we just could not allow ourselves to think that the word of God was also defiled. We thought that the Holy Spirit would filter on through, resulting in the truth we were to follow. And yet even the Bible refers to Satan as "the God of this world (aion) age". And that "age," characterized by the misery of war, poverty, child molestation and unspeakable horrors that have bedeviled mankind for as long as we have been recording history, has ended.

Many times you will see a statue of Baphomet in their art and literature. Whether you believe this religion or not is irrelevant because they believe it. They go way back to the Canaanites, descendants of Cain who worshiped Baal. Cain was the first murderer and from this culture came the practice of blood rituals, child sacrifice, and ritual abuse– spiritually, emotionally and physically. They believe that the younger they are, the more pure the blood which is extracted from the pineal gland and named Adrenochrome. They believe it to be the elixir of life and that it keeps them young looking into their 80's and 90's.

Another word to describe what these energy vampires do is lushing, the practice of gathering energy through our fear. The more terror that can be aroused in the victim enhances the adrenaline rush giving the blood a quality they very much covet. The terrorized victims are more controllable and very useful in their chosen vocation to further carry out the cabals' agendas.

Many went through the MK Ultra mind control experiments and became super soldiers where experiments having to do with transhumanism have been carried out for decades.

This Khazarian Mafia will never quit and certainly will not admit defeat. In light of that, Kim mentioned in early November 2022 that it has been determined that their energy is irreparable and cannot be redeemed. Humanity now has the cooperation of 125,000,000 ET's actively recycling these dark entities back to source for repurposing.

Our job is to continue to ground our energy and light to the planet and connect with our highest and purest source while we remove the energies interfering with our energetic fields. We consciously and verbally revoke our consent to all prior contracts of bondage while embracing our divine rights and expanding consciousness.

I have asked my higher self to reveal anything interfering with my energetic system and assist me with its removal as part of emancipating myself from the systemic Matrix.

Everything changes since the infusion of light to earth and this entering the new paradigm of Aquarius, characterized by the "water bearer." I think about water carrying memory, intelligence, electrical conductivity and its inherent life giving and life supporting properties. Water is said to carry information, and scientists like Dr. Emoto have shown that it also has memory. The "water bearer" information download is cleansing, and like any cleanse it can have the initial symptoms of a "healing crisis".

Our bodies are mostly water, but hydrogen holds 62% of the atomic structure, oxygen 24% and carbon 12%. Hydrogen will be one of the keys to restoring the health of the planet and ourselves, once we are rid of the contaminants in food production to allow proper digestion of hydrocarbons. In conjunction with electro-magnetic fields and anti-gravity, these suppressed resources will be part of our everyday lives. This clean free power will revolutionize travel and many other industries.

It is imperative that we prepare for the worst and yet hope for the best. Most farmers are very familiar with that old adage because in the event of a poor harvest, crop failure, drought or storms, all things that may or not occur, their very livelihood depended on it.

Have lots of candles and flashlights around the home in case of a power failure and of course water jugs or a method to catch the rainwater off a roof and a little propane stove to heat up food and water. Also you can buy freeze dried foods and large water storage jugs in the event of power outages and water shut offs from places like https://totalprepare.ca/ or just do a search for food prepared-ness or MREs (Meals Ready to Eat) in your region. Many people without a yard are buying Growing Towers which are excellent for some of the essential nutrients for life. Another new trend is grow-ing microgreens inside a room in your home, a relatively inexpen-sive way to grow healthy essentials.

Chapter 7

THE CLIMATE HOAX:
DIRECTED ENERGY WEAPONS

When the people fear their government, there is tyranny; when the government fears the people, there is liberty.

~ *Thomas Jefferson* ~

First the mainstream narrative was reporting on "global warming" until it was proven that the planet is actually cooling and has been going through cooling and warming cycles long before we were able to collect data. Next the narrative was modified to "global climate change" to cover their butts, without losing much momentum on the ruse. Now they're talking about global heating because "warming" actually sounds kinda nice. There is no "climate emergency," and it was way worse in the 30s and 40s according to Dr Judith Curry, Professor Emeritus and former chair of The School of Earth and Atmospheric Sciences at the Georgia Institute of Technology. This courageous and outspoken scientist has risked everything to bring us the truth and has given an interview at biznews.com.

First of all, science is never "settled," science is ever changing and evolving through hypothesis, experimentation and objective observation, concluding in evidence that may change by introducing new technologies and updated data.

Keep in mind that the ruling elite, intent on domination and control of the world, love to turn everything upside down, inside out and backwards, making evil into good and wrong into right. They are masters of deceit, trickery and word spell magic to such a degree that the greatest lie ever told has become a fear mantra repeated around the world by people of all cultures and faiths.

The two false concepts that the lie comprises are so pervasive and ingrained in our belief systems that they control every aspect of everyone's life, and the saying is, "There are only two things in life that are guaranteed, death and taxes."

There is no finality in death! Only a transition from one form to another as all matter is energy in motion and due to the Law of The thermodynamics energy, cannot be destroyed, it can only be transformed.

The High Priests of Babylon figured out the timetable for the recurring lunar eclipses, then easily convinced the masses that they controlled the heavens, thereby capturing unwarranted allegiances. The media today is more than adept at mesmerizing and captivating audiences worldwide.

Climate Change is a manufactured lie, designed toward a diabolical end that would ultimately destroy planet earth and her inhabitants. Why and who could possibly be on board with such nonsense? Do they not realize that their own families will fall victim to this wretched plan? Corrupt politicians who are in the know will have visited the D.U.M.Bs, Deep Underground Military Bases of which there are about 300 in North America. See Beforeitsnews. com for more information.

These are equipped with state of the art medical, dental and every other modern convenience desirable wherein they believe their families will have refuge. Blinded by money and power, they cannot see that their end will come when their usefulness has expired. There are thousands of similar bases and tunnels around the world that can be found through a simple search. Children born in these bases who are not sacrificed, are used in MK Ultra mind control experiments. U.S. veteran Gene Decode reports regularly on the D.U.M.B.s and shows how many of the earthquakes around the world are actually explosions carried out by "White Hat" military rescue operations for the children.

Many well-meaning people have been bewitched by the media propaganda machine and sincerely believe the world is in danger if we don't address this "climate crisis."

After the terrifying fires that wiped out Lytton, British Columbia, in 2021, a golfing buddy of mine shouted an inquiry to our foursome, "I guess there is no doubt about global warming now?" I knew it was meant for me, but I had no response that could be summed up in one or two sentences. I never was that good at thinking on my feet and did not want to get myself in trouble. There is evidence on the internet of people capturing events on their cell phones such as the California fires in 2019. They show how Directed Energy Weapons (DEWs), including high energy laser beams, microwave and particle or sound beams, were used to torch homes and automobiles while leaving the surrounding trees and vegetation in full bloom.

HAARP, the High frequency Active Aurora Research Project, is located at the closest point to the magnetosphere of the earth which is in Gakona, Alaska. It was originally introduced with the intentions for electrical grid application in the United States. But now with many more installations around the world, it is having serious consequences altering the ionosphere which protects all life from solar radiation. It is a series of large antennas used to beam radio frequencies for the use of communication, navigation and surveillance which sounds good, but it eventually came under the direction of the military and has been used for things like weather modification and Directed Energy Weapons. See Brighteon.com for a visual.

HAARP is beaming anywhere from 3 to 450 MHz or billions of watts/hour into the ionosphere and therefore it has a direct effect on the human body which also has a magnetic component primarily in our hearts and brains.[16] The awesome conveyor of our life force, the heart, resonates at 528 hz frequency.

The HAARP technology also allows for weather modification so that storms can be increased in intensity and directed to move over areas where they want to wreak havoc and create a situation like they did in Haiti. This opens the door to fund campaigns for organizations like The Clinton Foundation, to prey on the generosity of charitable donors, then launder the money while a tiny percentile actually helps the victims of their wrath.

These operations go on all the time and all over the world. A lot of the oil spills fall into this category and more recently the California and British Columbia fires. In Lytton B.C. that small community was burned down after the courageous Dr. Hoffe took a stand against our corrupt Health Minister Bonnie Henry. He was

---

[16] Angels Don't Play This HAARP: Advances in Tesla Technology by Nick Begich and Jeane Manning First published January 1, 1995

simply asking legitimate questions as to what protocols are in place to treat patients who have had serious adverse events.

The majority of Dr. Hoffe's patients in Lytton are indigenous people whose health has been seriously compromised after taking the "Clot Shot."

After that fire he then moved to his cabin in Monte Creek and were you able to guess? Oh yeah, another coincidental fire. But the brave men and women of that district didn't wait for the woefully tardy fire team to be dispatched by their controllers. No, the residents went into the belly of the beast and fought with shovels and axes and what limited water they could carry and were successful in saving their homes.

This type of action from local people is one way to demonstrate the principle of United Non Compliance. It is just too bad that it takes something as extreme as manmade fires, hurricanes, or the many other false flags such as the Covid pandemic, for us to act.

Since the beginning of our existence on earth we have pursued life and happiness in seeking to establish ourselves while exercising our inherent rights to food, water and shelter.

It becomes an assault on our primary instinct of self-preservation when livelihoods are destroyed, and people are threatened and enslaved and ultimately their lives are taken. To allow these criminals to continue to coral, muzzle, terrorize and lethally inject us is to deny our basic human rights to life, liberty and freedom.

Whenever we have reports of a "natural disaster," this red flag should alert you to do a little digging to discover who is benefitting from it and who is harmed? Does it fit with the globalist agenda? Use discernment and of course follow the money.

It has been shown in the recent data collected since the onset of the scamdemic that most vaccine injuries and deaths are among three primary races, those being Black, Latino and those native to their respective lands.

Also look at the disaster relief funds and who receives them, like in Haiti and New Orleans where actual people on the ground reported getting less than 5% of the donations.

Weather Channel founder John Coleman was an outspoken critic of the global warming theory. "It is the greatest scam in history," he said in 2007. "I am amazed, appalled and highly offended by it. Global Warming: It is a SCAM."

How many times have I been playing golf on a beautiful clear and sunny day when large plumes of smoke are spewed from jets many times headed upward on a 70 degree angle. I would have to ask what destination that aircraft could be flying to? The moon? By noon the skies would be gray and dismal and playing partners would deny my claims of the existence of "chemtrails." I informed them of the Environment Canada website where "chemtrails" are referred to as "geoengineering," It explained the reason was to block the suns rays to prevent the warming of the planet. No one cared that aluminum, strontium and barium, all harmful to biological life and highly flammable, were being rained down on us.

I mentioned earlier that "science is never settled" and alluded to the fact that it is in flux and evolving. There was a petition signed by over 30,000 scientists claiming that Global Warming is a Hoax and indicated that they reject the mainstream narrative. The list includes 9,029 PhDs, and they showed that human-caused global warming and consequent global damage was dramatically flawed.

Fact Checkers will counter this by discrediting these scientists and their affiliations. But the illusion breaks down when you see platforms like Facebook and Google use the so-called fact checkers to censor anybody on those platforms espousing contrary opinions to the mainstream narrative.

These scientists show how the hottest day in Australia on Record was in 1828 at *53.9 C 138F* just more proof that weather is cyclical throughout time.

Some say we are in another Solar Minimum period like the Maunder Minimum of (1645-1715 CE), or the Dalton Minimum of (1800-1824 CE). Cycles have varying recurrences from 200-year cycles to 600-year cycles and less where the global average temperatures on earth fluctuated as much as 2 degrees. All without any massive earth changes or any type of help from earthlings and especially with no efforts to tax populations which could somehow lower CO_2 emissions.

This is an absurd assertion by the political goons of our time to dupe the public into further enriching the elite, who fly their private jets into meetings like Davos where they discuss plans to keep us enslaved. Forbes magazine reported on the recent G20 Climate Summit in November. If all 118 private jets at COP26 flew an average of three hours to and from the event, that would put the combined carbon emitted by the 118 private jets at over 1,400 tons. But no worries, their propaganda machine will kick into gear using people like Greta Thunberg to control us and play on our guilt to make us comply.

How about their latest marketing efforts in favor of eating insects like caterpillars and grasshoppers rather than meat. When it didn't go over so well with people, they redirected our thinking to feeding our pets with these critters to gradually manipulate us into acceptance.

Combine all these with a digital ID tracking system for every human on planet earth, and I wouldn't put it past them to start taxing our farts. They are already claiming that methane gas from cattle is another cause of excess CO_2 emissions, and another stinking tax is about to be imposed on Australian farmers.

Do not underestimate their insanity as this "climate crisis" scare tactic goes viral much the same way as did the Certificate Of Vaccine Identification in 2019.

Chapter 8

THE MEDICAL FRAUD:
REVEALED BY A HEALTHY FEAR

*"The germ theory of disease is the greatest travesty on 'science'
that was ever stumbled over during this semi civilized age; the
most ghastly medical farce in which the human mass ever played
its part; the biggest hoax the medical profession ever took in after
but little hesitation and no mastication."*

~ *The Germ Theory by Royal E.S. Hayes, M.D.* ~

I t is not obvious to everyone that our health is directly influ-
enced by what we ingest, rather the belief system of most is to
rely on their doctor to care for the many symptoms that plague
us throughout our lives. This bandage approach takes responsibility
for one's health from each individual and transfers it to the trusted
physician for ongoing treatment with very little collaboration to
arrive at a complete healing.

My former wife Sheri and I started to become aware of the
medical health fraud back in the early 90s as we were raising our
three beautiful daughters. We became more health conscious as we

discovered that many of the products in our grocery stores were not only unhealthy, but downright dangerous to the human species.

Still we didn't make the connection that all systems are corrupt, or at least not to the extent that we now know.

We were sure that spraying our crops with herbicides and pesticides could not facilitate the absorption of nutrients into our bodies. But it wasn't until I visited an organic farm in Ohio and the farmer told us that the insects only eat the weaker plants so the grower is left with only the most nutritious of foods to take to market. Similar to how in the animal kingdom, a lion will seek out his prey and cull the weak and injured from the herd. Of course large food corporations are not concerned with these concepts, rather greater quantities of lesser nutritious value yield greater profits. So the solution back then and to some extent today was to buy organic, although that industry is now being compromised as well. Watch for buzz words on product labels like "natural flavoring" which usually means some form of monosodium glutamate (MSG).

Also the meat production and slaughtering process has been compromised to produce profits above quality.[17] Cattle of all kinds are driven mad by being kept in cages for months before going to the slaughter house, and all that fear and adrenaline in their blood is not the type of energy that is conducive to human digestion. So best to find a local farmer in your nearby farmers market where you can form a direct relationship and access organic meats, dairy and vegetables.

And for our weekly shopping a very handy App which rates the nutritious value of the product simply by scanning the Barcode can be found here: https://app.yuka.io/2EJzggvxak8T6vyr5.

---

[17] Natural Cures They Don't Want You To Know About Kevin Trudeau

They were not successful in completely destroying the natural health movement, but they were able through universities and regulatory bodies to license and control them. Now anyone claiming anything outside of the medical mafia's regulations can be fined and/or have their licenses revoked, thereby denying a livelihood to those practitioners.

You may know that the medical establishment more than frowns upon any product or person who claims to heal anything or anyone. As a matter of fact many alternative health practitioners have had early deaths because they persisted in publishing their work and making their methods known. You are actually not allowed to use that word healed under the medical model's jurisdiction because it is counterproductive to managing symptoms via numerous treatments which systematically produces a lifetime client.

This is how the controllers muddy the waters mixing actual remedial processes with concoctions that give temporary relief of symptoms. They have no intention of ever finding a cure for cancer, which there already are many, because it is a multibillion dollar per year cash cow.[18]

Now please don't get me wrong as I am well aware of the benefits of many of the services offered by allopathic medicine, such as a surgery for a broken limb and/or certain drugs needed in many cases. I myself had a month-long stay in hospital after a horrendous head-on collision with a car that somehow happened to be on our side of the highway. I needed an immediate surgery on my right tibia, but my left heel was smashed in 40 pieces, and that foot was the size of a football, so that 15-hour surgery was not possible until the swelling went down. Then there was the 3rd degree burns on my right shin from the fire that started while I was stuck in my

---

[18] https://www.leafly.ca/news/cannabis-101/what-is-rick-simpson-oil

vehicle. The dermatologist consulted with me to figure out which thigh would be the least intrusive to get the skin graft from to patch up the shin. Now I wear a 1inch lift in my left shoe as that leg was shortened by the impact. I mean, I'm very fortunate to be alive and most grateful for those doctors and their teams for their expertise and care for me during that time. I'm sure that most doctors go into the profession motivated by a sincere desire to help people and learn the fascinating science involved in knowing human anatomy and discovering new cures for disease. Ah, but few know that the industry has been co-opted by these monsters with plans and goals for global control in every facet of mankind's existence.

The practice of Chiropractic and Naturopathic healing modalities has also been controlled by licensing and regulators. The herbalistic industry was demonized and suppressed while vitamin supplements were downplayed and given a bad reputation in well-respected medical journals. Especially after the Rockefellers discovered how to use all types of oil by products in pharmaceuticals and made a huge push in advertising to ready the market for the production and distribution through the medical system. Their control system includes influential board members being shuffled around between hospitals, universities, regulatory institutions, key political positions, as well as the Big Banks.

In the early days of smelting and refining aluminum, there were excessive amounts of the by-product fluoride and dumping it into the rivers was soon frowned upon as being a viable option. So they commissioned studies from the Universities they fund to bring about the necessary findings, to quell the growing opposition to this hazardous waste. Later requirements consisted of editing textbooks and updating educators with the latest "science" at those same universities. Now bring in the big advertising companies and with everyone on the same page, they teach in Dentistry and the related medical fields how fluoride is beneficial to our teeth and overall health. It is a very difficult task to convince a dentist or her accompanying hygienist of the harmful and longlasting effects of fluoride. They have spent years being "edumacted" and years using and recommending the product, so to do an about face is so contrary to their programming and almost requires a spiritual awakening, or maybe a 2 by 4 across the brow would work.

Many more are now becoming aware of this fraud simply because of the widespread so-called "pandemic" which has been exposed right from the beginning to those who were paying attention. Thank goodness for the plethora of lawsuits, documentation, testing and information available, so now only the completely brainwashed, still glued to the mainstream media are captivated by the ruse.[19]

Regarding our overall health and wellbeing it has been accepted widely across most cultures that Germ Theory would be the basis for diagnosis. But that theory has been debunked, due to the volumes of research published in favor of Terrain Theory, so much so that the latter is no longer referred to as a theory.

Now please do not rush over to the mainstream controlled media such as Wikipedia, where objective research is not supported. It will not refer to the death bed confession of the germ theory founder Louis Pasteur, who renounced his lifetime work in favor of the work of his friend, physiologist Claude Bernard. Bernard taught that the terrain of the human body was more important than the 'pathogens' that infect it. Another word for terrain is "environment" and therefore "garbage in, garbage out!"

---

[19] https://librti.com/uninformed-consent

There are trillions of viruses in the air, water, earth and our bodies at all times and they play an integral part in these living ecosystems. Our air, water and earth are intentionally polluted, and the environment inside and outside our bodies has everything to do with our wellness. Unlike the germ theory, the terrain theory explains why some people get sick while others, when exposed to the same pathogens, do not. For this reason, it is said that on his deathbed, Pasteur admitted, "Bernard was right: the pathogen is nothing, the terrain is everything."

Canadian physician Dr. Andrew Moulden provided clear scientific evidence to prove that every dose of vaccine given to a child or an adult produces harm. The truth that he uncovered was rejected, covered up and discredited by the conventional medical system and the pharmaceutical industry. Nevertheless, his warning and his message remains as a solid legacy of the man who stood up against big pharma and their program to vaccinate every person on the Earth.

Dr. Mouldens died unexpectedly in November of 2013 at age 49. Hmm! See *The Terrain* by Ray Andrew, MD.

Because of the strong opposition from big pharma concerning Dr. Moulden's research, we became concerned that the name of this brilliant researcher and his life's work had nearly been deleted from the internet. His reputation was being disparaged, and his message of warning and hope was being distorted and buried without a tombstone.

More than 100 years ago, Rudolf Steiner wrote the following:

"In the future we will eliminate the soul with medicine. Under the pretext of a 'healthy point of view', there will be a vaccine by which the human body will be treated as soon as possible directly at birth, so that the human being cannot develop the thought of the existence of soul and spirit. Materialistic doctors will be entrusted with the task of removing the soul of humanity. As today, people are vaccinated against this disease or that disease, so in the future children will be vaccinated with a substance that can be produced precisely in such a way that people, thanks to this vaccination, will be immune to being subjected to the "madness" of spiritual life. He would be extremely smart, but he would not develop a conscience, and that is the true goal of some materialistic circles."

With such a vaccine you can easily make the etheric body loose in the physical body. Once the etheric body is detached, the relationship between the universe and the etheric body would become extremely unstable, and man would become an automaton, for the physical body of man must become polished on this earth by spiritual will. So the vaccine becomes a kind of arymanique force; man can no longer get rid of a given materialistic feeling. He becomes materialistic of constitution and can no longer rise to the spiritual". Rudolf Steiner 1861-1925.

The term "Follow the money" will more often than not help us find the truth to many well-hidden agendas. Consider the enormous profits made throughout the medical system on pharmaceuticals, hospital care, and ongoing treatment because the model is based on repeat business, not on curing ailments.

The cancer industry alone produces multi billions of dollars annually, never mind the multitude of diseases and so-called chronic illnesses doing likewise. I do not mean to insult anyone who is currently dealing with such an illness, my intent is purely to bring awareness to issues of injustice and harm committed on humanity. Just imagine if the trillions spent on drugs and treatment were spent on truly finding a cure. We would eradicate most every disease and be very healthy throughout our consequently long lives.

Some of the many harmful ingredients that agencies like Health Canada and the FDA allow are aspartame, monosodium glutamate (MSG) fluoride, and be very wary of the deceptive term "natural flavors" which is very often just MSG.

Fluoride is common in many water systems and yet the active ingredient in Prozac Fluoxetine, is made up of 18.5 percent fluoride and is a neurotoxin that dumbs you down.

Even in the NIH National Library Of Medicine there are Independent studies linking aspartame to memory loss, and a significant increase in several types of lymphomas and leukemias in rats, as well as causing painful fibromyalgia and formation of formaldehyde in the body and much more.

The money trail leads us to the agendas which reveal their sinister eugenics plans for control. Can you imagine if Hitler had announced his depopulation agenda? It was only after millions of people disappeared that his eugenics program was discovered, and people around the world have been appalled and disgusted ever since.

Today they are lining up for "safe and effective" vaccines just as they did in the death camp gas chambers, thinking they were going for a shower. Notice the huge rise in chronic disorders in the last 50 years, in things like Autism, Allergies and Autoimmune Deficiencies. All these diseases should have been diminishing with the knowledge and technologies of our modern day, instead they throw more money away to the same institutions that created the problem.

The difference today is that the Luciferians' influence has permeated every aspect of modern culture, so much that their arrogance is much more "in your face!" I'm referring to that Ted Talk in Chapter 4 where Gates actually is very open about how to remove 5 billion people from the planet to solve the world's carbon problems. It bears repeating that Gates and his cohorts George Soros and Klaus Schwab are planning this eugenics operation over the next decade. These plans include vaccines, health care and genetically modified food, leaving them with a very manageable population of slaves.

Another one of their partners in crime who is actively creating these bioweapons is Anthony Fauci, Director of NIAID since 1984. He does all this within the government funded portfolio of basic and applied research to prevent, diagnose, and treat established infectious diseases such as HIV/AIDS. This little devil oversees the creation of viruses in laboratories then has them placed in vaccines to proliferate their eugenics programs around the world.

Dr. Judy Mikovits used to work alongside this maniac thinking she was researching the effects of the AIDS virus and developing an antivirus to combat the problem. She discovered the nefarious plans of Fauci, but when she brought the information to light her career was ruined and she spent time in jail as a result.[20]

The entire AIDS epidemic was another one of their many plans to depopulate the earth with undesirables. Their modus operandi is 1) Problem 2) Reaction 3) Solution. First they have a desired effect or outcome, i.e.: depopulation, then they create a scenario usually based in fear and guilt that would cause an outcry from the people to do something. And finally they present their formerly planned solution which fulfills their agenda.

---

[20] Https://odysee.Com/@projectcamelot: d/dr.Mikovitsanddr.Young-re-vax_final:8

For example, create a fear and guilt program through their controlled media to mesmerize folks in Africa and India that a deadly virus outbreak from monkeys is attacking their immune system and causing deaths. They have already created this acquired immunodeficiency syndrome (HIV/**AIDS**) in the lab to be introduced into the vaccinations. After a quarter million children were murdered in each country they kicked Gates, Fauci and their damn vaccines out and filed lawsuits.

They should be getting a taste of their own medicine as of October 10, 2022. The excerpt below from Ben Fullfords' newsletter expresses the beginning of their downfall.

Ben is a Canadian investigative journalist who used to work for Forbes Magazine until his truth style reporting kept being rejected by the publisher. He now works privately out of Japan, and he opened this week's newsletter with: Worldwide shoot-to-kill orders have been issued against all Khazarian Mafia members until they surrender unconditionally, according to an agreement made between MI6, the CIA, Mossad, the Russian FSB and other military/intelligence agencies worldwide. This is legal and in self-defense because the KM are actively trying to kill 90% of humanity. If they surrender, they will face Nuremberg-style war crimes tribunals. If they don't, they face death. Individuals targeted for immediate execution include the actors pretending to be President Joe Biden and Pope Francis, Jeff Bezos, Jared Kushner, Justin Castro (Trudeau), Chrystia Freeland, Emanuelle Macron, Ursula von der Leyen, Angela Merkel, Anthony Fauci, Albert Bourla, Bill Gates, the Chief Rabbi of New York Ephraim Mirvis etc. We will ask our readers to help compile a more comprehensive list, but this is a good starting point. You can sign up for Ben's weekly newsletter at www.benjaminfulford.net.

Wow such good news for all who have been waiting so long to bring these criminals to justice and we watch as this part of the reality we are experiencing comes to fruition.

Also in the news is Evelyn De Rothschild, representing the French arm of the central banks, who died at the age of 91 on the night of the Blood Moon November 8, 2022. In other news another Rothschild who represents the Swiss banking arm, Klaus Schawb, has been neutralized, and Germany has left NATO, strong indicators that the Rothschild reign of terror has come to an end. It's looking like the United States and Canada will be the final strongholds to fall.

To add to that Kim Goguen announced on UNN in early November that it has become crystal clear that the lack of cooperation from the remaining members of the Cabal is because their energy is so dark that they will never change. Some say the White Hats Military are responsible for the take down, but time will tell.

Chapter 9

THE CERTIFICATE OF VACCINE ID 19: SCAMDEMIC

"I must confess that I am tempted to ask for reincarnation as a particularly deadly virus."

~ *Prince Phillip, duke of Edinburgh*

Isn't it telling how the name COVID 19 for the non-virus was introduced right at the beginning of the "pandemic"? Even though the non vaccine had not surfaced yet and we were still two years away from the "Vaccine Passports". It was never about a virus or a vaccine but rather a method to digitally track every human activity on planet earth. This method is complete with medical history and linked to our bank accounts utilizing a New World Order digital currency.

This Digital Credit System can then add or subtract credits based on your compliance with Draconian orders. The sociopaths make the laws to ensure the protection of the few in power and to the detriment of those they rule over to the point where they decide that you are no longer useful to their society and you can simply be turned off to fend for yourself. I can only imagine the horror of that situation.

Here in Canada they are pushing the Arrive Can App which is to hold all your vital information from health to banking to tax data based on the model presently being used by the Chinese Communist Party in China. This system is complete with facial recognition cameras on every street, and in every building, not just airports, government establishments and border ports.

At this writing freedom loving patriots are crossing into Canada without the Arrive Can App on their phones because the border agents have no authority to enforce this unlawful practice. The so-called Health Authority of Canada cannot lawfully detain anyone, yet we still see long lines of fearful people who have no idea of their rights and

liberties. But the learned patriots courageously walk past the queue daring to set themselves apart based on their rights of informed consent under The Nuremberg Code and Section 11 of the Quarantine Act of Canada. Again, like any bully, once you take a stand, the coward will back down and maybe even try to hand you a ticket with an extremely high dollar amount, which most, if not all of these, were thrown out of the courts. Oh, and mandates are not laws, and normally require the agreement of both parties and encompass employment. As far as I am concerned a mandate is two guys meeting for coffee.

Unified Non Compliance should be our mantra going forward with regard to masks, testing, social distancing, lock downs and especially the clot shot. Yes, that's right, it does produce blood clotting leading to all kinds of heart conditions and a myriad of other maladies and death. Each shot and booster further weakens the immune system until it is completely diminished. The installed operating system leaves you no defense other than to continue the shots in order to stay alive.

On a brighter note there are many remedies that can and do help if you are not too far along in their process such as Hydroxy-chloroquine and Ivermectin treatments.

Quinine has many uses and applications, and it is no wonder our governments medical institutions and health ministers, paid by big pharma, are banning it under the guise of being ineffective. Dr. Peter McCullough, the most peer reviewed doctor on the planet, is being demonized for speaking about his well researched findings on the pandemic.[21]

Quinine has enjoyed widespread use for decades as an analgesic, anesthetic, antiarrhythmic, antibacterial, antimalarial, antimicro-bial, antiparasitic, antipyretic, antiseptic, antispasmodic, antiviral, astringent, bactericide, cytotoxic, febrifuge, fungicide, insecticide, nervine, stomachic, and tonic.

The safety of Hydroxychloroquine (HCQ) is irrefutable. The evidence supporting HCQ efficacy against Covid-19 is also over-whelming. All negative HCQ studies have used either: too much, used it alone (it needs Zinc), or used it late (it should be early.) The dosage recommended by doctors worldwide is 200 mg HCQ twice a day for five days + Zinc 50 (elemental) daily. The prophy-lactic dose doctors recommend is 400 mg HCQ weekly + Zinc 50 (elemental) daily. (There are studies right now to see if HCQ 200 mg. weekly is sufficient.) This is a very low dose. (The usual dose of HCQ in Lupus, Rheumatoid Arthritis is 400 mg. daily for years.)

---

[21] https://rumble.com/v1l1o4z-dr.-judy-mikovits-and-dr.-peter-mccullough-weigh-in-on-corruption-within-th.html

If you ever feel a chest cold coming on or just feel like crap, make your own Quinine. It's made out of the peelings of grapefruits and lemons but especially grapefruit and here is the recipe below. Make tea out of it and drink it all day. Take zinc with this recipe which propels the quinine into your cells and brings faster relief. Take the rind off of 2-3 grapefruit, the peel only, and cover it with water 3 inches above the peels. Put a glass lid on it or a metal one if you do not have glass and let it simmer for about 3 hours. Do not take the lid off the pot until it cools completely as this would allow the quinine to escape in the steam. You can sweeten the tea with honey if you find it too strong. Take 1 tablespoon every couple hours to bring up the phlegm in your lungs until you feel better.

The World Council for Health (WCH), a worldwide coalition of health-focused organizations and civil society groups that seek to broaden public health knowledge, has released a spike protein detox guide, which provides straightforward steps you can take to potentially lessen the effects of toxic spike protein.

Anti-inflammatories, exist and may be useful for those seeking to detox from COVID-19 or COVID-19 injections:

Boswellia serrata (frankincense), Dandelion leaf extract, Black cumin (Nigella sativa)Curcumin, Krill oil and other fatty acids, Cinnamon, Fisetin, Apigenin, Quercetin, Resveratrol, Luteolin, Vitamin D3 (with vitamin K), Zinc, Magnesium, Jasmine tea Spices, Bay leaves, Black pepper, Nutmeg, Sage.

Doctors have shown how Ivermectin, for example, docks to the SARS-CoV-2 spike receptor-binding domain attached to ACE2, which may interfere with its ability to attach to the human cell membrane. They also compiled a list of spike protein neutralizers, which render it unable to cause further damage to cells. This includes:

- N-acetylcysteine (NAC)
- Glutathione
- Fennel tea
- Star anise tea
- Pine needle tea
- St. John's wort
- Comfrey leaf
- Vitamin C

The plant compounds in the list above contain shikimic acid, which may counteract blood clot formation and reduce some of the spike protein's toxic effects. Nattokinase, a form of fermented soy, may also help to reduce the occurrence of blood clots. These are just some of the many remedies for these toxic cocktails being pushed on humanity to attain their goal of population control and Eugenics. China's one child quota is a small part of the agenda.

Even our doctors have been deceived who only know Ivermectin as a horse dewormer and have not looked at the volumes of data and decades of use in curing many ailments. The fact is that Merck developed it for humans first at a much lower dose than a horse gets, and it was so cheap and effective that it was later found to be used for animals very easily and effectively.

Maybe there are some doctors who actually still think they are "following the science" because they haven't done the research themselves and they are obedient to their corrupt health authorities. Just like the public was bribed with lottery tickets and treats for kids, physicians and hospital officials were blinded by the multiple payments they got for each shot and booster. They also receive payments for every PCR test and the hospitalization of victims as well as the further harmful administering of treatments like ventilators, Remdesiver and Diazepam which bring in thousands of dollars.

It was Dr. Kary Mullis, Nobel Laureate in Chemistry, who created the PCR and said that it was not to be used for diagnosis, but it allowed scientists to create millions of copies of DNA molecules. In other words, whatever is showing in the blood the PCR will make a whole lot more of it which results in a whole lot more false positives, and he recommended running it between 20-25 cycles, but the health authorities have been operating the PCR tests at 30-40 cycles. Dr. Mullis was another one of the many outspoken adversaries of the medical mafia and the coward Fauci always declined when challenged to a debate. Professor Drosten later developed the PCR into a test to diagnose infection contrary to its original design.

In Denmark they have banned the vaccine for youth under 18 and have announced that people under the age of 18 are no longer allowed to get the COVID vaccine.

Those wanting their first shot were cut off after July 1, 2022, and no one in the age group – aside from those who are considered "high risk" and have a doctor's note – will be allowed to get a second shot after September 1, 2022.

While many are likely relieved because it means that vaccine mandates won't be coming back to school, few countries have followed Denmark's lead, and if the science is universal, it's a wonder why they haven't.

For example, despite this decision from Denmark, babies are now eligible to receive three rounds of Moderna's Covid vaccine in Canada, even though COVID poses no greater threat to babies than the flu does, and Health Canada admits they lack long-term safety data.

Moreover, various health authorities have recently highlighted the risks of adverse effects that exist from the COVID vaccines.

While it seems that more and more authorities are warning of the risks of vaccines – which, according to Denmark, are greater than the risk of COVID for the young and healthy – few countries are willing to say outright that the risks outweigh the benefits.

Pfizer did not want their analysis of Adverse Events released for 75 years, of course by then most of their victims would be dead and the rest of us would be under full government control. They hoped their analysis of Adverse Events would remain proprietary and confidential, but the courts made them release it to the public domain.

5.3.6 CUMULATIVE ANALYSIS OF POST-AUTHORIZATION ADVERSE EVENT REPORTS OF PF-07302048 (BNT162B2) RECEIVED THROUGH 28-FEB-2021

Report Prepared by: Worldwide Safety Pfizer; the information contained in this document is proprietary and confidential.

The report is based on the Pfizer vaccine trial, cumulatively, through 28 February 2021, there were a total of 42,086 case reports (25,379 medically confirmed and 16,707 non-medically confirmed) containing 158,893 events.

Wow! This bioweapon should never have made it to market and the list of adverse effects is an extensive 9 pages long with an insane summary and conclusion. It reminds me of the lists of side effects we find on prescription bottles, although those lists pale in comparison.

See the Summary and Conclusion below and just a snippet of the Appendix on page 1.

5. SUMMARY AND CONCLUSION Review of the available data for this cumulative PM experience, confirms a favorable benefit: risk balance for BNT162b2. Pfizer will continue routine pharmacovigilance activities on behalf of BioNTech according to the Pharmacovigilance Agreement in place, in order to assure patient

safety and will inform the Agency if an evaluation of the safety data yields significant new information for BNT162b2.

APPENDIX 1. LIST OF ADVERSE EVENTS OF SPECIAL INTEREST 1p36 deletion syndrome;2-Hydroxyglutaric aciduria;5'nucleotidase increased; Acoustic neuritis; Acquired C1 inhibitor deficiency; Acquired epidermolysis bullosa; Acquired epileptic aphasia; Acute cutaneous lupus erythematosus; Acute disseminated encephalomyelitis; Acute encephalitis with refractory, repetitive partial seizures; Acute febrile neutrophilic dermatosis; Acute flaccid myelitis; Acute haemorrhagic leukoencephalitis; Acute haemorrhagic oedema of infancy; Acute kidney injury; Acute macular outer retinopathy; Acute motor axonal neuropathy; Acute motor-sensory axonal neuropathy; Acute myocardial infarction; Acute respiratory distress syndrome; Acute respiratory failure; Addison's disease; Administration site thrombosis; Administration site vasculitis; Adrenal thrombosis; Adverse event following immunization; Ageusia; Agranulocytosis; Air embolism; Alanine aminotransferase abnormal; Alanine aminotransferase increased; Alcoholic seizure; Allergic bronchopulmonary mycosis; Allergic oedema; Alloimmune hepatitis; Alopecia areata; Alpers disease; Alveolar proteinosis; Ammonia abnormal; Ammonia increased; Amniotic cavity infection; Amygdalohippocampectomy; Amyloid arthropathy; Amyloidosis; Amyloidosis senile; Anaphylactic reaction; Anaphylactic shock; Anaphylactic transfusion reaction; Anaphylactoid reaction; Anaphylactoid shock; Anaphylactoid syndrome of pregnancy;

95% of deaths today are among the vaccinated. The funeral director from the UK, John O'Looney, controversially claims there were no excess deaths in 2020. "The reality is the death rate only soared the moment they began putting needles into arms in January 2021."

He should know, and I don't know about you, but I'm hearing many more sirens these days from the first responder ambulances and have noted in many news reports that it is not just the elderly getting sick and dying but people of all ages, and far too many are our young folk.

And how about all the athletes who are dropping on the soccer and football fields, tennis courts and ice rinks. The most common diagnosis is myocarditis, and pericarditis especially in young men, and they will deal with this for the rest of their probably shortened lives.

Then there is the covert attack by this bioweapon on future generations via sterilization. These will become more frequent in the coming months and years as the bioweapon carries its patented technology throughout the bloodstream affecting every organ of the body down to the cellular level.

The vaccine was patented before the virus, and oh, I thought that nature could not be patented which means one of two things. The virus is not natural, or the patent is illegal.[22] And why would you patent the supposed treatment before the existence of the very thing being treated becomes evident? Hmm! Follow the money just like Dr. David Martin whose company has been investigating patents since 1999 and has uncovered the origin of the Corona virus patent and its illegality, and he has no problem exposing the blatantly evil motivation for this occult bioweapon.

Here is what the Center For Disease Control (CDC) lists on their website: Myocarditis is inflammation of the heart muscle.

Pericarditis is inflammation of the outer lining of the heart.

• In both cases, the body's immune system causes inflammation in response to an infection or some other trigger. Learn more about myocarditis and pericarditis.

---

[22] Dr. David Martin 9-13 minutes https://www.bitchute.com/video/4u7rt61YeGox/

- Both myocarditis and pericarditis have the following symptoms:
- Chest pain
- Shortness of breath
- Feelings of having a fast-beating, fluttering, or pounding heart

Myocarditis and pericarditis have rarely been reported. When reported, the cases have especially been in adolescents and young adult males within several days after the mNRA COVID-19 vaccination (Pfizer-BioNTech or Moderna).

- More often after the second dose
- Usually within a week of vaccination
- Most patients with myocarditis or pericarditis who received care responded well to medicine and rest and felt better quickly.
- Patients can usually return to their normal daily activities after their symptoms improve.
- Those who have been diagnosed with myocarditis should consult with their cardiologist (heart doctor) about returning to exercise or sports.

There are many protocols issued by front line Doctors who have a genuine desire to help their patients which you can research at www.twc.health. The prestigious Salk Institute has authored a bombshell revealing that the SARS-CoV-2 spike protein is what's actually causing vascular damage in covid patients and covid "vaccine" recipients, promoting the strokes, heart attacks, migraines, blood clots and other harmful reactions that have already killed thousands of Americans.

"Critically, all four covid vaccine brands currently in widespread use either inject patients with the spike protein or, via mRNA technology, instruct the patient's own body to manufacture spike proteins and release them into their own blood." This mRNA technology seems to function like an operating system.

This floods the patient's body with the very spike protein that the Salk Institute has now identified as the smoking gun cause of vascular damage and related events (such as blood clots, which are killing many people who take the vaccines). Researchers learned about shikimic acid, a plant phytochemical that's touted for reducing platelet aggregation which may stop the vascular damage in Covid patients and Covid "vaccine" recipients?

There are at least 3 foods in the plant kingdom that contain relevant levels.

1. Pine
2. Fennel
3. Star Anise.

So Pine Needle Tea or Pine Needle Essential Oil can be helpful.

Fortunately we have a highly qualified committee of lawyers, doctors and unbiased scientists led by Dr. Reiner Fuellmich, who is conducting a Grand Jury to bring these criminals to justice. These concerned professionals are not being paid to promote the mainstream narrative and below is a link to the Video and Full Transcript of Dr. Reiner Fuellmich's presentation.

Reiner Fuellmich, October 7, 2020

The German Corona Investigative Committee has taken testimony from a large number of international scientists and experts since July 10, 2020.

See this brief outline of their findings

- The corona crisis must be renamed the "Corona Scandal"
- It is the greatest crime against humanity ever committed and those responsible must be criminally prosecuted for crimes against humanity and be sued for civil damages

- Doctors and hospitals worldwide were paid to declare deceased victims of Covid-19
- Many scientists call this a PCR-test pandemic, not a corona pandemic
  - Prof. Drosten developed his PCR test from an old SARS virus without ever having seen the real Wuhan virus from China
  - The lockdowns were based on non-existent infections
  - Mainstream media completely failed to report the true facts of the so-called pandemic
  - Politicians and mainstream media deliberately drove populations to panic
  - Children were calculatedly made to feel responsible "for the painful tortured death of their parents and grandparents if they do not follow Corona rules"
  - Evidence of gigantic health and economic damage to populations
  - Anti-corona measures have:
    - Killed innumerable people
    - Destroyed countless companies and individuals worldwide
    - Bankruptcies are expected in small- and medium-sized businesses
  - A class action lawsuit must be filed in the USA or Canada, with all affected parties worldwide having the opportunity to join
  - Companies and self-employed people must be compensated for damages

Reiners Updates September 28, 2022 http://t.me/ReinerFuellmich

I was encouraged by Reiner Fuellmichs' statement in his videos that he is well aware of the corruption in the justice system and the reason for the Grand Jury. The evidence should produce criminal indictments but after that remains to be seen.

Watch this interview with Dr. Reiner Fuellmich and Dr. Peter Breggin. https://www.brighteon.com/d32165a1-f1c9-40c2-974d-33c0c8ef50c6

Dr. Breggin is a renowned psychiatrist and physician, and an outspoken critic of the current psychiatric system. Dr. Breggin considers modern psychiatry to be a materialistic fraud that takes an overly simplistic approach by medicating patients with all sorts of problems that have their roots in causes other than brain chemistry. He and his wife Ginger have written the book *COVID –19 and the Global Predators: We are the Prey.* A very comprehensive study and very affordable on Amazon for everyone at $2.99.

Another very pertinent lawsuit here in my home country of Canada has the unique characteristic of the participation of the last remaining signatory to our Constitution and Charter of Rights, the Honorable Premier Brian Peckford who was Premier of Newfoundland for ten years.

The case is regarding the travel mandates that restricted 6 million Canadians from traveling domestically and to foreign countries. The Ministry of Transportation has yet to provide any proof that the unvaccinated are more dangerous than the vaccinated, and that they pose any risk to travelers, hence the travel mandates have no bonafide justification.

His affidavit of evidence went uncontested by the Crown because they didn't choose to cross examine him, and our brilliant lawyer for the people, Keith Wilson, K.C. says that under court rules it basically means no cross examination equals the evidence is accepted as fact.

Of course you know that I do not place a lot of faith in the system because the legal system is infested with parasites all the way to the top. But even still many are looking forward to winning these cases, putting faith in our creator and the global consciousness. We hope that not all of the justice system has been compromised and they know in their hearts what is right, so the possibility of a favorable outcome is still within our grasp.

Another interesting Canadian case involves The College of Physicians and Surgeons[23] and how they hi-jack our well-meaning doctors with coercion, threats and bribes.

If you only have ten minutes, start with Canadian cancer specialist and groundbreaking cancer researcher Dr Makis. His ten-minute testimonial starts at 19:00 and ends at 29:00. Dr Makis' story shows how corrupt and criminal these organizations were even before they started their current role in the gross violence that is the covid mafia crimes against humanity.

I recently became aware of some very highly qualified doctors who are fed up with the systematic destruction of their profession and have opened their own wellness centers at https://www.twc.health/ to address patients' health issues on a cash basis.

---

[23] https://drtrozzi.org/2022/09/27/colleges-of-physicians-surgeons-rampant-criminality/

Chapter 10

THE UNIFIED FIELD: AS IS HELP FROM ABOVE SO IS HELP FROM BELOW

"The beauty and the scent of roses can be used as a medicine and the sun rays as a food."

~ *Nikola Tesla* ~

Our mother earth is surrounded by an electromagnetic field and ideally synchronized with our own individual field. Our aura expands outward more than 6 feet and every time we come in contact with anyone, our auras intermingle and there is an exchange of which most of us are aware. Not only that but our consciousness is connected to the Unified Field and is transmitted across continents and beyond. Some people you are attracted to for a multitude of reasons, and others not so much. This is where getting in touch with our intuition is very helpful in directing our energy towards a healthy and abundant life as it was meant to be. When we are together it behooves us to interact with each other using our humor, intellect, emotional and spiritual selves to enhance our lives by nurturing our friendship and love for one another.

Dr. Steven Greer[24] is one of the world's foremost authorities on the subject of UFOs, extraterrestrial intelligence and technologies, and initiating peaceful contact with interstellar civilizations. He gave up a very good career as Chairman of Emergency Medicine at Caldwell Memorial Hospital in Lenoir, North Carolina. His research shows that our Milky Way Galaxy has at least 10,000 earth-like civilizations. Let that incubate for a minute or better yet, meditate on it and imagine the possibilities the future holds for man/womankind.

Some of these civilizations are millions of years ahead of us in technological development and have found it necessary to intervene in our affairs according to intergalactic law. According to these Universal laws, they are only allowed to directly interfere with us, in order to prevent harm to other galaxies. For example the detonation of nuclear bombs where the explosions would reverberate out into the Universe. Consent is necessary and we can ask for their help also, which I keep very simple and in conjunction with my higher self.

When the megalomaniacs in power on earth began tests by shooting nuclear devices into the stratosphere we received help from above, and they intercepted the missiles extinguishing them so as not to expose the universe to a harmful nuclear detonation.

The concept of extraterrestrial beings in other galaxies on other planets should not be too alarming to earthlings at this stage of our development. There are some whose eyes will glaze over at the mention of the topic and the more religious types believe they are all demons. But to think we are the only intelligent sentient beings in the never-ending sea of the multiverse is quite self-centered and immature. Naysayers would do well to watch the link on Dr. Greer

---

[24] https://www.brighteon.com/00000000-0000-0000-0005-841925263001

or get one of his books which are loaded with live testimonials from very creditable military and three letter agency people.

Eventually our medium of exchange will develop into a new monetary system, a quantum system, until we learn more about harnessing and utilizing the energy from the Unified Field to manifest our basic needs to benefit humanity.

Scientists and inventors have created devices that draw the water right out of the atmosphere to plumb an entire house. And there are new technologies such as BioGeometry which uses the energy principles of geometrical shapes to balance biological energy systems within the overall framework of the environment. BioGeometry is the only science so far that has been effectively applied on a wide scale for the harmonization of the effect of electromagnetic fields (EMFs) and geopathic stress (Earth energy grids) on biological systems. See Dr. Ibrahim Karim, Founder of the Science of BioGeometryelds and geopathic stress (Earth energy grids) on biological systems.

There are many free, clean technologies that have been blacklisted at the patent offices for decades even going back to the time of Nikola Tesla. He excitedly brought news of his "Wardenclyffe Tower" that would provide wireless transmission of electricity, based on alternating current, to his financier J. P. Morgan. But when Morgan realized it would devastate his copper mining and he wouldn't be able to put a meter on it to bring in a monthly revenue, he decided to go with Edison's direct current model instead. This is the type of thinking that has plagued us and kept us enslaved to a system that not only robs our pocketbooks but also steadily erodes our health, which feeds into the medical treatment modality for repeat business.

Tesla also proved that the earth, with its electromagnetic field, is a conductor resonating at about 8hz, yet he was never given credit when it was later acknowledged and named The Schumann Resonance.

If you would like a more detailed look into Nikola Teslas' drawings, patents and life send an email to kirk_450@protonmail.com and I will email you the pdf. file.

Creative inventions along with new ways to do things like farming and manufacturing will reduce the time necessary to do specific tasks as we work towards the global goal to bring about a 16-20 hour work week for everyone. For instance, anything that can be produced locally will make massive shipping operations across oceans and continents obsolete.

People will rotate in and out of different tasks pertaining to the fi elds they choose to participate in based on their level of knowledge and expertise. Products will be made with only the highest quality materials and will last for decades, requiring little to no maintenance which will free up more time to create, explore and pursue happiness. Th is is an oversimplified explanation just to give you the idea, but with the advent of new technologies like "Med Beds" the need for long hours on the operating table will be dramatically reduced.

And this is only the beginning because we are in the process of learning how to use plasma within consciousness entangled with zero-point energy to heal ourselves. See The Keshe Foun-dation.

It has to do with memory being equated with time and how the cells in our body have memory. A person inside a med bed, where let's say an arm severed at the elbow will have a hologram of his whole arm, hovering in place in its perfect prior shape all the way down to the fingers. The cell memory at the point of incision recognizes their former perfection from the hologram and begins the healing process to bring that body part back into harmony with the whole. The same process can be done with organs and virtually any other body part needing repair. In 2012 I began practicing this within my own primitive understanding and applying the meditation principles of visualizing to strengthen my left foot. I also attribute much of the healing to my use of Advanced Nerve Formula from www.realhealthproducts.com because it rebuilds the damaged myelin protective sheath around each nerve. Today I am able to walk and play golf with relative ease and only minor discomfort at times.

Pretty much every new revolutionary idea and the proponents of them fell into the definition of quackery until proof of their effectiveness became self-evident. Some of the many inventors are the Wright brothers, Galileo, Nikola Tesla and Einstein to name a few. Even Newtonian Physics took 20 years before it was accepted, although that is being challenged now by Quantum Physics.

And of course it has always been the same families and monarchies desperately demanding control labeling them as "nut jobs." And in the middle ages, "witches" and heretics were tarred and feathered or burned at the stake. Rather than taking an intelligent and mature attitude embracing new ideas and technologies, exploring and experimenting to prove or disprove, they quickly jump to fear driven conclusions to maintain their illusory power.

Another one of the many environmentally friendly projects was started by a young innovator Boyan Slat of https://theoceancleanup.com/ who has created the Ocean Cleanup, a non-profit organization, developing and scaling technologies to rid the world's oceans of plastic. He states, "Our aim is to put ourselves out of business once the oceans are clean." Boyan is another example of the kind of service to others attitude that will be displayed more as we go forward into the new millennium and young innovative minds become free to explore and develop their ideas and technologies.

People will have the liberty to follow their dreams without the intervention of complex regulations that stifle growth and experimentation, keeping in mind the Universal Natural Law, "Do No Harm."

There will be a place for everyone as menial tasks will be performed by robots and or the many people who are perfectly happy to be of assistance as they move into differing areas of a particular operation or profession. And those who are highly skilled in the necessary arts and sciences will be governed by their passion to continue in those endeavors perfecting and teaching their craft. Studies have shown when children are asked what they want to do, they pick high paying occupations but when told that they have unlimited funding they almost always choose humanitarian projects.

Kim, who I mentioned before, is the Guardian of the global accounts and in control of the back end of this quantum system. She is no longer funding the corrupt governments, militaries and corporations as did her predecessor. Even now she is tirelessly working on gaining access to the front end of that system of which the Cabal is gradually losing their grasp. She has proven to them that she is "Ground Command" by sending one dollar to their accounts and making an offer to include them in the global funding if they cooperate. Since she is no longer funding them, she made an offer in October 2022 to the top corporations in the world, Vanguard and Black Rock, to buy them out now that they are headed for a colossal bankruptcy. If their plan was to succeed, they would have allowed the rest of the world to go bankrupt while they swooped in like a hawk, surprising its prey and devouring each business and corporation much the way it happened in 1929.

See the insert showing the mind staggering number of companies that they control:

She told them she was going ahead with the restoration of planet earth with their cooperation or not, and I for one do not think they will agree because it goes totally against their nature. Picture the school yard bully, who is intercepted by a teacher and is told to give back your phone, so angered that he was discovered he then "accidentally" drops it on the ground with a smug attitude that exudes, "If I can't have it no one can."

Already we have the Vielight 633 Red Light therapy which is a simple, non-invasive treatment that delivers red and near infrared (NIR) light to the skin and cells. It optimizes cellular function to improve overall health, and some have used this personal photobiomodulation device for their cancers.

The ideological model is in the dream stage at present but as we develop a new system of energy exchange which does away with the current broken monetary model based on lack mentality, humanity will be freed up to explore our creative nature.

Once the reality of an abundant mindset has found its roots in our makeup, people will develop their extra sensory abilities and cooperate in harmony with each other and the universe at large.

We will create the world of our desires based on tapping into the universal consciousness which is our subconscious mind located in our solar plexus. This is where our parasympathetic nervous system interacts with our cerebral nervous system. The harmonizing of these minds does not mean we lose our individuality, on the contrary, it allows us through mutual support and cooperation, in alignment with the Law of Attraction, to develop our abilities to the fullest.

In my own profession, High Rise window cleaning, the business model is based on repeat business simply because things get dirty over time and need to be cleaned. I still believe that a device can be created to disintegrate the molecules of soil on a surface and veritably activate those molecules to dissolve the debris. Something in the manner of how water can turn to steam then evaporate into thin air. I know it sounds next to impossible, but if I can think of it, I know it can happen based on my experience and because our global consciousness is immersed in the quantum Unified Field always interacting with itself.

Long before we had squeegees that swiveled and ladders with leveling jacks on the legs of the ladders, for uneven ground, I thought about them. I even tried to make drawings, and looked into the long drawn out and complicated legal process of patenting. But once again for the little guy running around struggling to build a business and raising three girls, the system makes it very difficult financially and legally to pursue.

It's mostly the large corporations with resources and technology already in the manufacturing of many products who bring out the new tech, and in a few years, I was enjoying the benefits of said products. Some inventors who have a formula or specs on a new device that threatens an existing technology can have their ideas held up at the patent office indefinitely if the creator cannot be bribed. Even worse, if the creators continue to search for alternative means to bring about their invention and especially if it is a revolutionary product, they are just eliminated.

Stanley Meyer, rumored to have been poisoned, is one such inventor who created a car powered by hydrogen from water. The basic principle is this: molecules have a positive and negative magnetic side. Normal electrolysis can use the magnetic principles of water to rip it apart, but it uses a ton of energy.

If the exact resonant frequency of the water is used, along with special circuitry that multiplies the voltage, while reducing the amperage to as little as possible, the resonant frequency will cause the water molecule to temporarily "elongate".

A normal oxygen molecule has 6 electrons, but can hold up to 8 in its stable state. That makes it accept the 2 electrons of the hydrogen atoms. When the water molecule elongates, it allows the hydrogen atoms to be separated from the oxygen atom very easily. In turn, this produces "hydroxy gas, called "Brown's Gas" or "HHO, which are basically forms of hydrogen and oxygen.

We certainly need hope and faith in our eternal and ever present allknowing highest and purest source. Call it God or Source. Call it the Life Force, or whatever your preference.

When I ponder the intricacies of the human mind and form, and the wondrous interactions of the earth, I think, "surely the foundations are under laid with an intelligence beyond my imagination."

I was not able to grasp any of the "Big Bang Theory" and so began to run the gamut of being a truth seeker from about age 13 when I asked my parents, "what is the meaning of life." As you might expect they gave me a very indoctrinated answer about getting a good education, so as to acquire a well paying job and finding and marrying a lovely girl with which to raise a family.

My immediate instinctive response was "that's not it" and it was apparent they too did not know. Thus my quest for spiritual enlightenment led me down the path of self-discovery and an ever expanding awareness of the multiverse and its creator.

It's probably why I was unable to submit to the school system and did not resonate with it other than making friends and playing sports. I saw no value in continuing past the secondary level having acquired my grade 12 Diploma.

I was first attracted to and began reading about Buddhism and Hinduism because of the mystical attraction of eastern wisdom. I was reading works like Siddhartha by Hermann Hesse and the writings of Kahlil Gibran which were popular in the 60s, along with the peace love and groovy slogan during my rebellious "hippie" days.

I'm not sure if I have Attention Deficit Disorder (ADD) or what, but I have always seemed somewhat distracted with a limited ability to pay undivided attention to any one thing for an extended period of time. It could be because I think in pictures more than words, so when attempting to meditate I wasn't able to sit still and stay focused on breathing long enough to reap the benefits. Maybe it was part of the alcoholic personality or the trappings of being in my twenties, but today I am more willing to take the time to explore that aspect of metaphysics.

In any case, I am making a concerted effort at connecting to the creator and cleansing, shielding and communicating mostly via visualization and grounding the light of the highest and purest source.

Meditation may be one of the best ways to seek the illusive blissful state, although more often than not, all too many people seek that state of being via ingesting drugs and alcohol. I am very familiar with that form of temporary relief from the trials of life and the downward spiral of destruction that follows. But we are all attracting our reality and there is talk of food replicators becoming available in our lifetime. Ultimately, we will learn how to manifest our needs and desires, not only for the individual benefit, but for the uplifting of all consciousness.

And yes, many great and wonderful truths were left in the Bible because like everywhere that the Cabal infiltrated, there must be some truth to sustain some credibility. But it is well known by ardent students of biblical research that mainstream churches have had their doctrine corrupted and watered down. One of the most glaring examples is that of allowing governments to tax them. The usury laws are not confined to Christianity, they are prevalent in most all religions and yet they are flagrantly violated everywhere.

Now I know they will defend their position by quoting from Romans where it states, "render to Caesar what belongs to Caesar." But that sticks out like a sore thumb amidst the many other places where it is forbidden. Especially if they give credence to the occurrences where the messiah entered the Temple in a rage and overthrew the tables of the money changers (banksters).

I won't go into the many law vs. grace arguments here, because there are multiple inconsistencies too numerous to go into, but suffice to say that the King James Version was commissioned by a sodomite who murdered his wife and child. To believe that it is the most revered translation of the Septuagint, which was held in high esteem as the best Greek translation of the Aramaic text, is simply naive. The Summerian text is the basis for the belief that man is 6000 years old but many other texts such as The Emerald Tablets show man and the earth as 13.5 billion years old. I recently became aware of the highly knowledgeable and very articulate Billy Carson who explains, "we are a walking hard drive" and we are the Universe, as literally all information for all time is stored within each and every one of us. Peer reviewed scientists have found that there are 700 terabytes of information in 1 drop/gram of human DNA which includes all our years of existence.

Another best-selling author, Gregg Braden, has shown in his many years of research that our human DNA has a code that is written in Aramaic, Hebrew and Sanskrit. He and his team were able to decipher this code in each language and discovered the same words, "God eternal within the body." How fascinating and utterly delightful to contemplate the unfathomable depths of wisdom and enlightenment in this knowledge.

The whole "end times" scenario has been co-opted by the Luciferian cult full of all the things they love like war, famine, pestilence, virus causing diseases and death. Now insert the return of Christ to come save his people from the apocalypse while the rest of humanity goes to hell. This is a doctrine embedded in the Christian psyche designed to render them waiting to be whisked away in the twinkling of an eye, rather than them coming to the realization that salvation comes from within.

"The only thing necessary for the triumph of evil is for good men to do nothing." Edmund Burke

But what if it is the Christ Consciousness that is actually returning? Empowerment of everyone as we awaken to our true destiny and take control of the direction we are headed. Now with the Eternal God within we become the savior we were waiting for and do the works that he did, and even the greater works that he said we would do.

Have you heard of Project Blue Beam? A back up plan if too many of their other plans fail where they can project holographic images of whatever suits their needs. One narrative that has been discussed is a fake alien invasion where the whole world is convinced via media hype to get on board for a New World Order cooperative to defeat them. Remember their motto, "Order Out of

Chaos" and imagine how much death and destruction they could revel in during that kind of ruse.

Another scenario is the previously mentioned return of Jesus on a white horse in the sky showing over many of the major cities to dupe Christians into following their long-awaited leader into whatever demise the Cabal have in mind.

"Fortunately some are born with spiritual immune systems that sooner or later give way rejection to the illusory world view grafted upon them from birth through social conditioning. They begin sensing that something is amiss, and start looking for answers. Inner knowledge and anomalous outer experiences show them a side of reality others are oblivious to, and so begins their journey of awakening. Each step of the journey begins with following the heart instead of following the crowd, and by choosing knowledge over the veils of ignorance." Henri Bergson 1859-1941

As I alluded to earlier, the Red Pill is particularly difficult to swallow and unlike the movie The Matrix, it is not an instantaneous transition from a life of pretending that everything is just fine to a realization that we are not in control. But wait! Now that we have digested the Red Pill, we become aware that we do have the power to manifest our reality and we are responsible for the world we see today.

Quantum physics has proven that all the information in the universe, for all time, exists in every human. We are all a part of this Unified Field of consciousness, and everything is recorded in the field and affects the field, so our individual decisions make a difference. But the quality of our decisions is based on our subconscious training acquired during our formative years when the subconscious mind can only record without judgment, all our experiences. And to the extent that the quality of the program came from people who had learned to love themselves, then the play back recordings for the rest of our lives carries the baggage of our parental training. It matters not how well meaning they were simply because they were merely playing back their own subconscious recordings.

We can also learn so much on the subject of epigenetics by Dr. Bruce Lipton and his illuminating study of how to reprogram our formative subconscious and truly love ourselves. In these fascinating studies he talks about the use of positive affirmations via headphones to reprogram the subconscious while in the Theta state just before falling asleep.

Everything in the universe functions within a Unified Field and is constantly in a toroidal motion which is made up of extremely tiny plancks, a fundamental universal constant that defines the quantum nature of energy and relates the energy of a photon to its frequency. These plancks are billions of times smaller than a proton according to Nassim Haramein. And he says the source of the gravitational field, the source of the electromagnetic field and the source of mass can be thought of as a fluid running through everything. He explores his findings with the founders of the Thrive Movement Foster and Kimberly Gamble. In this segment he and Foster go over some of his findings. https://rumble.com/v1pna4j-part-1-foster-gamble-and-nassim-haramein-unified-field-trip.html

Listen to the fascinating mind of Nassim Haramein on Sacred Geometry And Unified Fields.

https://www.bitchute.com/video/seT923AWEckz/

The Unified Field where everything is one has always been and will always be and is past present and future all at once which some call the space time continuum. The field is all knowing, existing in a blissful state of joy, and decides in its infinite wisdom to separate itself into parts of many more than quadrillions of cells. Each cell is alive and complete with neutrons and protons and a nucleus that interacts with all the other cells in a toroidal sphere of communication continually expanding and exploring and looping information back to itself as it grows.

In simple terms the fundamental structure is energy full of life, and that life is abundant with light, color and sounds that continue to expand and grow and create within itself.

Every cell is sovereign, but it resonates with the other cells and unites to bring about harmonious sounds and colors which further enhances their relationships and comprehension.

Then this intelligent, beyond our imagination, cellular structure divides and creates duality, secure in the knowledge that the very blueprint for its foundation is the Life Force and therefore continually growing and thriving.

It will shelve its memory through the process so as to conceal the outcome from itself and when the time is right, triggers inherent in that blueprint begin to awaken the consciousness. Germination begins the ultimate growth from out of the darkness of the soil to a beautiful thriving being reaching up for the light.

The duality is to experience all possible outcomes even into the depths of darkness and the illusion of death, humans reincarnating and ever gaining more knowledge of self. The supporting Life Force by its very nature cannot be destroyed and will continue to evolve and eventually emerge with full comprehension of its blissful self once again.

With the dawning of the new age, 26,000 years of oppression and the planet being under quarantine are behind us, and now we begin to claw our way out from the cocoon of our existence to a new dimension that nurtures the manifestation of our wings.

The mystics tell us that our missing DNA is gradually being plugged back in and our pineal gland is being decalcified. It has been "dumbed down" as a result of the many contaminants we ingest.

Now we move from 3rd density to 4th and on up to 5th density vibration ever increasing in our extra sensory abilities. This is all new to me, but I am enjoying the ride experimenting with some of the simple practices like "cloaking" or becoming invisible. Situations arise where one does not want to be noticed, maybe in a crowd or at an event, and I just command that I am free to move about as I wish without drawing attention to myself. Some refer to this gift as cloaking, which may become more necessary, especially because our auras are becoming more full and radiating the energy of love, which brings us more in harmony with the universal mind.

The law of attraction presents people, circumstances and situations more favorable to our growth and the enhancement of our overall well-being. We are harmonizing with the orchestra of the cosmos and our lives are playing a very special instrument unique and tailored specifically to each one. Every time a soul awakens and begins their integral process, another part of the whole puzzle allows for a greater vision individually and collectively.

One thing to always keep in mind is the fact that almost everything we are told in the mainstream is either upside down, inside out or backwards. That is to say, question everything because we are being lied to continually as one of the many mechanisms of control.

For instance, recently I took a look at the sunscreen I use especially since I would see a lot of golfers with their faces plastered with a whitish cream giving them a very unnatural ghoulish look. After taking a look at the ingredients I easily discovered several very harmful ingredients such as parabens and UV filters. Most of them contain hazardous petrolatum and propylparaben or benzyl salicylate, a fragrance identified as an "established contact allergen in humans" by the European Scientific Committee on Consumer Safety.

Now I use Shea Moisture 100% Extra virgin Coconut Oil without fragrance allergens or any other detrimental ingredients to keep from skin burning while golfing.

Remember how our well-meaning parents told us to "never look directly into the sun?" Well that is only partially true. We do not want to look or gaze at the sun other than the two times when it is not only safe but beneficial to do so. The first hour our sun peaks over the horizon and the last hour while it diminishes in the west are "safe and effective" to use the modern-day nomenclature.

When I began this practice, I could only look directly into the sun for about 30-60 seconds, but as I became more accustomed to it, I found I could go for several minutes and enjoyed the effects.

I love anything that is counter to the propaganda of the day because it is most likely to be true and it is a simple formula for discernment, although care needs to be taken as much disinformation can easily muddy the waters.

Proponents of Sun Gazing can be found at <u>www.solarhealing.com</u> where you can read all about it if you are interested.

CONCLUSION

"Grapes must be crushed to make wine. Diamonds form under pressure. Olives are pressed to release oil. Seeds grow in darkness. Whenever you feel crushed, under pressure, pressed, or in darkness, you're in a powerful place of transformation and transmutation. Trust the process."

~ Tiny Buddha. ~

We are witnessing the collapse of the evil cabal, deep state, Khazarian Mafia with the recent deaths of some of their leaders like the Queen, Evelyn De Rothschild, and even Henry Kissinger is looking like he is on his last breaths.

The 3.5 percent rule states serious regime change can be brought about with nonviolent protests, and our world population at present is close to 8 Billion. We outnumber them by the billions and only need about 280,000,000 people for the machinations of evil to be made obsolete. United Non Compliance and our efforts to bring the various freedom loving people and groups together will go a long way to healing the planet and her people.

Put your mark or autograph on the consent page of The Global Peoples Monetary System at gpms.world and let us unite to manifest and be the change we want to see.

ABOUT THE AUTHOR

Kirk Galbraith was born and raised in Toronto, Ontario, Canada where he lived for 41 years before moving his family to Kamloops, British Columbia.

After discovering that he did not fit in the corporate world he developed his own window cleaning business. He sold the business due to Covid restrictions after operating for 30 years.

He always had a fascination with spiritual matters and the metaphysical which led him to 40 years of research and study that culminated in *The Art of Conspiracy.*

Made in the USA
Middletown, DE
18 March 2024

51704194R00077